Praise for *Heart in Tatters*

Heart in Tatters adds depth and dimension to the stories of people who became presidents, congressmen, and key military figures, bringing to the forefront Eunice Tripler's enormous contributions to the life and career of her husband. She endured lengthy separations from him, often raising her children alone or with scant help, and took on a bureaucracy in defense of her husband and family. As the descendant of a Civil War veteran, I am gratified to see the contributions women made to that "new birth of freedom" being recognized. Eunice Hunt Tripler is a prime example from which to begin.
—**Nancy Hancock** is a history author, blogger who gives lost stories a voice, preservationist, and self-described historical entrepreneur

This volume enables us to hear the voice of a woman, and her words reveal the experience of the Civil War through a gendered lens, one we don't often get to see through. This perspective prompts the reader to think about the Civil War and the experience of war in new ways. This exciting inaugural volume stands as a tremendous contribution and sets the stage for the series of MCWA publications to follow.
—**Dr. Martin J. Hershock**, historical author, Dean and Professor of History at University of Michigan-Dearborn

During the Civil War, military wives did more than keep home and hearth intact while their husbands fought hundreds of miles away. Some of those fiercely proud and determined wives insisted on meeting with President Lincoln during the Civil War to urge him to promote their husbands in the U.S. Army. Eunice Hunt Tripler did that—and much more. Her story, told in this first volume of the MCWA's projected series, launches this project with candid insights into some of the war's most famous men and fascinating details of life during that era that I have not seen anywhere else before.
—**Candice Shy Hooper**. Historian, author of the award-winning *Lincoln's Generals' Wives: Four Women Who Influenced the Civil War for Better and for Worse*," contributor to the *New York Times*' "Disunion" blog

Most accounts of the American Civil War focus on the battles and men of the times. This compelling book from a woman's point of view recounts Eunice Hunt Tripler's experiences and interactions with many influential people. She was an eyewitness to this crucial period of history. Many of the issues of her time still resonate in America. As a first-person performer of historical women, I find Mrs. Tripler a fascinating woman worthy of wider renown.

—**Bonnie Johnson**, co-founder of Historical Echoes, current chair of the Amelia Earhart Birthplace Museum Board of Trustees

In this inaugural publication of the Michigan Civil War Association, I was privileged to be introduced to a remarkable woman who had a front-row seat to the social, political, and military challenges of this tumultuous time. Eunice Hunt Tripler was an astute observer; her description of the city of her birth, Washington, D.C., and the politicos who populated it (for example, a surprisingly warm-hearted Andrew Jackson); the many military leaders she encountered (including "that old humbug Gen. Scott") after marriage to an Army doctor; and her own experiences raising children in Detroit during such terrifying events as a cholera outbreak while her husband served a thousand miles away were both pointed and poignant. This book would be a welcome addition to the shelves of anyone who enjoys reading about the lesser-known stories surrounding the Civil War, especially works by or about women who contributed to the preservation of the Union in their own unique ways while confronting the social mores of the time.

—**Patricia Majher**, author of *Ladies of the Lights: Michigan Women in the U.S. Lighthouse Service* and *Great Girls in Michigan History*, former editor of *Michigan History* magazine, former assistant director of Michigan Women's Hall of Fame (now Herstory Museum)

Eunice Hunt Tripler's detailed and accurate recollections of her well-connected life before and during the war are enlightening and entertaining. The MCWA has done a real service to Civil War scholarship in publishing these lively and forthright memoirs.

—**Dr. Gerald J. Prokopowicz**, professor of history, East Carolina University, host of Civil War Talk Radio

Eunice Hunt Tripler's delightful memoir is a valuable resource for historians of the mid-19th century and fascinating reading for anyone interested in America's past and its key figures, many of whom Tripler knew personally.

—**Dr. Steven E. Woodworth**, professor of history, Texas Christian University, prolific Civil War author

HEART IN TATTERS

HEART IN TATTERS

Eunice Hunt Tripler

and

the Civil War

MICHIGAN CIVIL WAR ASSOCIATION

© 2022 Michigan Civil War Association
All Rights Reserved

All world rights reserved

No part of this book may be reproduced, stored in a retrieval system, or transmitted in any form or by any means electronic, mechanical, photocopying, recording or otherwise, without the prior consent of the publisher.

Readers are encouraged to go to www.MissionPointPress.com to contact the author or to find information on how to buy this book in bulk at a discounted rate.

Published by Mission Point Press
2554 Chandler Rd.
Traverse City, MI 49696
(231) 421-9513
www.MissionPointPress.com

ISBN: 9781958363416
Library of Congress Control Number: 2022917929

Printed in the United States of America

★ ★ ★

Proceeds from this volume benefit the Michigan Civil War Association in preserving and sharing Michigan's role during the American Civil War.

At the time of this publication, the MCWA is raising funds to erect a monument honoring Michigan's contributions to victory and to emancipation at the Battle of Antietam,

Sept. 17, 1862.

★ ★ ★

The Michigan Civil War Association is a Michigan 501(c)(3) non-profit corporation.

Its corporate purpose is to pursue cultural, historical, and economic development opportunities to preserve and promote the history of Michigan's role in the American Civil War.

Founded in 2013, the MCWA has acted as a careful steward of all donations received.

More information is available at https://www.facebook.com/michigancivilwarassociation.

★ ★ ★

Board of Directors
Bradley M. Egen
Kalamazoo

Brian James Egen
Monroe

Will Eichler
Washington Township

David D. Finney Jr.
Carmel, Indiana

Margaret O'Brien
Portage

Matt Van Acker
Lansing

Jack Dempsey
Plymouth Township

Publications Committee
Margaret O'Brien
Matt Van Acker
Jack Dempsey

Editorial Consultant
Dr. Martin J. Hershock
Dean of College of Arts, Sciences, and Letters
Professor of History
University of Michigan-Dearborn

Contents

Preface xi
Introduction & Editorial Note xv
Memoirs of Eunice Hunt Tripler 1
Historic Sites 97
Appendix 99
Postscript: The Female Union Doctor 109
Bibliography 113
Index 117
Acknowledgments 122

Illustrations

1. Washington in 1820s–1830s 43
2. Detail from Rotunda painting showing Eunice Hunt 43
3. Etching of Eunice as young woman 44
4. City of Detroit, 1837 44
5. Eunice as young married woman 45
6. Fort Gratiot—current photo of post hospital 45
7. Newport Barracks 46
8. Seven Buildings (where Eunice helped with paperwork) 46
9. Charles S. Tripler in uniform 47
10. Eunice as older woman 48
11. Cover or first page of Manual 49
12. Grave, Elmwood 50

Dear Washington, how I love you, with your beautiful, broad, generous streets and blue skies! The sun shines always there for me.[1]

---

1. *The Personal Memoirs of Julia Dent Grant*, John Y. Simon ed. (New York: G.P. Putnam's Sons, 1975), 327.

Preface

History matters. History is relevant. When the Pew Research Center conducts a study on trusted institutions where people can obtain reliable and accurate information, libraries rank number one with museums a close number two. Foundational to any serious publication of a historical work, libraries and museums, that often contain rich historical archives of primary source information, are crucial. These rich reservoirs of knowledge are treasure troves of past ingredients that can illuminate our roadmaps to help navigate today and tomorrow.

Unfortunately for many, their experiences with history derive from elementary and high school social studies where a potentially less than enthusiastic instructor compelled memorizations of dates, facts and figures. While these are important, without the context and connection to the human element with relevancy to their own lives, they are sterile and uninspirational, leaving a cultural abyss in our shared understanding and appreciation of our collective story.

It is often said that those who do not learn from the past are doomed to repeat the same mistakes. As events move beyond living recollection of the generation who lived those events, collective memory and understanding disappear. This generational cycle runs between 80 to 100 years. Subsequent generations, who lack the acute personal memories of firsthand experiences, tend to jettison those stories without understanding the consequences of doing so – exposing the real threat of recurrence. That is not to say that people should harbor the mistakes, failures, and negative sides of the past to create a brighter future but having a respectful understanding of and being open to history will provide, in an uncanny way, a benchmark to greater inform us in events and circumstances we encounter. In a rudimentary way, it is like a pitcher who learns a batter's past hitting tendencies to determine how best to pitch for success.

The Strauss–Howe generational theory articulates this phenomenon in not only American but world history wherein historical events relate to "recurring generational personas…in which each unleashes a new era where new social, political, and economic climate exists." In short, when that persona's long "human life" passes, so to do the memories of events only to be replaced by new ones of the current generations. Thus, the loss of relative experience and learning from those foregone events.

All too often the casual assignation with the past falls short of a complete and balanced narrative that is productive. Instead of embracing the past as a model to learn and be inspired, we frequently castigate the past as rendered by a less-informed or enlightened generation. This deprives us of the true benefit of history.

I often hear how history is past and not relevant to one's life today. Even a cursory examination of life today reveals an extraordinary and bountiful cache of current events that refute that claim; a claim that is not only for a few but nearly everyone. Whether it is individual state's autonomy and rights versus a strong federal government, the balance of power in our legislative and judiciary branch, challenges and interpretations to the constitution and its amendments, personal autonomy and civil rights, educational reform, foreign affairs policy, energy, and more (the list goes on and on), it ALL has precedent in our past, our history.

Whether comparing current events such as the COVID-19 pandemic with the 1918 Spanish Flu or investigating the uncanny similarities of the current eastern European military conflict to September 1, 1939, precedent found in the past is undeniable. The comparisons and mentions to history, beyond people's living collective memory, of the January 6, 2021, U.S. Capitol events to the War of 1812, the Confederate flag passing through under the painting of leading 19th century abolitionist Charles Sumner, and a whole host of other parallels proves we are irrefutably tied and connected to our past. Though needing curation to meet our current circumstances, history provides many lesson plans for us to examine and use in our navigational journey.

The awareness and exposure to history should serve as an inspirational touchstone to fuel us in our lives today. It should sustain us and provide motivational nourishment in our own advocations and causes. The triumph of the human spirit, the tenacity of American grit, the sacrifice for a higher cause, the ordinary doing the extraordinary, the achievement beyond the unachievable, and so much more can be a source that touches that secret place of awe in each of us and compel a better tomorrow.

History, as it has been written and expressed, has been predominately the showplace of significant events, people, and places with the lesser-known stories and voices, often overshadowed. Over the past couple of decades, greater research, and stories of the oft-neglected or relegated voices, have emerged and become made more widely shared. It routinely comes to light that these heretofore unknown or feebly told histories are true underpinnings of significant events and the whole cloth fabric of our history.

This is a tremendous amount of power and responsibility that historians possess. Though history is about the past, it was never intended for those who have passed. It is about our lived experience, it is about our connections, it is about our story to inspire a better future. It is vital to keep the important circumstances, lessons, and events from the past within our intellectual and emotional grasp to help frame the world. This is exceptionally true of history beyond our living memory.

The Michigan Civil War Association's purpose is to share Michigan's stories of sacrifice, contribution, and impact during the Civil War era. Exploration of the military, social, political, and economic histories of Michiganders, especially those whose stories may have been traditionally marginalized and previously under-told, will be shared and available. The MCWA's publication division greatly serves this aspect of our mission in this, the first of what is planned to be a continuing issuance of new publications that are designed to raise money, such as for the Michigan Monument at Antietam, by sharing great, untold, and underappreciated stories about Michigan Civil War history. We hope this lesser-known story of Eunice Hunt Tripler will inspire you. Her fascinating story and work with her husband, Dr. Charles Stuart Tripler, provides great insight to their contributions to both the martial and civilian field of medicine in the mid-19th century that have impacts relevant to modern day practices and processes.

Please permit history to be an influence in your life. Apply the inspiration to your own advocations in life and learn from the past to help better your future and those with whom you share it. We appreciate your support and thank you for your interest in this publication. Let history ignite that spark.

Tuebor!

—Brian James Egen
President, Michigan Civil War Association

Introduction

The life of Eunice Hunt Tripler remains a fascinating story after the passage of more than a century. Born in 1822 with notable lineage, she lived to the age of 87, a witness to momentous events and personalities during the decades in which Americans disputed and then took up arms in the Civil War over democracy and human bondage. Her recollections of those individuals comprise a veritable *Who's Who* of famous names. Her marriage to a renowned physician, the first medical director of the largest army in American history, adds to an account worthy of notice in its own right. Mother to nine children, she would one day confront the possibility of losing her husband and a son who commanded Union troops in combat. Her resoluteness is remarkable during a lengthy life. As she phrased it, "In view of all the changes I have lived through I often feel as though I belonged to a former age of the world." Those years began with the last Revolutionary War veteran serving as U.S. President and ended during the era of Teddy Roosevelt. Born in Washington, D.C., her loyalty to the Union, not secession, not slavery, never flagged.

Because of the social circles of her parents in both Washington and Michigan, the young Eunice came to know a host of politicians and officers whose fame would largely derive from the ramp-up to and conduct of the American Civil War. Winfield Scott was a familiar presence. Her husband served in the Mexican-American War with many whose names became familiar – Lee and Johnston – and similarly in California – Grant and Hooker, and marriage brought them, and others such as Sherman, into her circle. Both Triplers came to know Ulysses S. and Julia D. Grant in Detroit. Both of them were present in

Washington during the early months of the Civil War where, among other celebrities, their paths crossed that of Abraham Lincoln. His encounter with the President embarrassed the otherwise stolid physician; hers happened coincidentally when she paid a visit, without his foreknowledge, to his commanding officer in order to lobby for the doctor's greater authority. She also encountered Mary Todd Lincoln at a White House event. Each episode reveals much about her personality and the vibrant marriage of an extraordinary couple. Her boldness in advocating her husband's causes demonstrated love, loyalty, and a certain liberation.

Eunice's nearest ancestry included patriots of the early decades of the independence of the United States of America. Her birth and youth in Washington, D.C. brought contact with heroes of the American Revolution and Presidents of the still-new nation. Her family's move to Detroit enabled association with memorable personages of that growing city in the Territory of Michigan. It also made possible an introduction to a military man who was sixteen years her senior. Within months, they would be wed and launch an epic love story marked by much poignancy. Her father died of an accident precipitated by his military service when Eunice was sixteen. Of her nine children, five predeceased her, with three dying as infants. Her husband's death at age sixty-six, when she was forty-four, tore away her lifetime companion. She never remarried.

With his wife's contributions, Dr. Charles Stuart Tripler fashioned a sterling military career that included service under fire in the Mexican-American War and the War of the Rebellion. Whenever the doctor's military career took him away from home, she had to manage family matters as the sole parent in place. Her personal safety was placed at risk, but she responded courageously. His reputation in both civilian and martial spheres led to appointment as the first Medical Director of the Army of the Potomac. He was among the central staff who aided Major-General George B. McClellan, "the Little Napoleon," in building a disorganized and unhealthy mass of green recruits into a formidable fighting force. He led the provision of medical care during that Army's famed Peninsula Campaign from March-July 1862. After that assignment, he continued to provide important medical services to Union soldiers in the Midwest. Without his leadership, DMC Harper University Hospital in Detroit would not have begun with sponsorship as a soldiers' recovery facility. It served patients regardless of race. It continues to provide medical care after a century and a half.

Eunice Hunt was born in Washington, D.C., on October 11, 1822, the eldest of six children.[2] Her parents, Thomas Hunt (born in 1791 or 1794) and Alice Forsyth (born in 1803 or 1804), were married in Detroit on September 29, 1821. Her father, third oldest of ten, served in the War of 1812 as a young commander and fought at the Battle of Brownstown near Monroe.[3] His health suffered after being taken prisoner-of-war at the surrender of Detroit. He became an officer in 1813 and rose to Captain in 1824 before resigning in October 1836. He died on February 17, 1838, Alice a half-century later on June 18, 1888.[4] They were interred in Detroit's Historic Elmwood Cemetery.

Thomas's father, Thomas V. Hunt, born in Watertown, Massachusetts, on September 17, 1754, had enlisted in Captain Croft's Company of Minutemen and fought at the Battles of Lexington and Concord on April 19, 1775, when he was twenty years of age. He served in other units and was wounded in the Battle of Stoney Point on July 16, 1779, and again at the culminating Battle of Yorktown in 1781. After the Revolutionary War, he married Eunice Wellington of Waltham, Massachusetts, and attained the rank of Colonel in the

---

2. Other notable Civil War-related 1822 births: Mathew Brady*; Ulysses S. Grant; Edward Everett Hale; Rutherford B. Hayes; Dabney H. Maury; Frederick Law Olmsted; John Pope; Fitz John Porter; George Stoneman; George Sykes; Harriet Tubman*; Joseph N.G. Whistler [* marks a debatable date). Also, the year of Denmark Vesey's Rebellion.
3. Le Roy Barnett & Roger Rosentreter, *Michigan's Early Military Forces* (Detroit: Wayne State University Press, 2003), 113.
4. *Senate Committee Report No. 96*, 36th Congress, 1st Session; *Return of Deaths in the County of Wayne, 1888*, 41.

U.S. Army.⁵ In 1800, he was commandant of the garrison at Detroit and, in 1802, he served as commandant at Fort Mackinac.⁶ He died on August 16, 1808, age fifty-three. His grave, and his wife's, lie in the Jefferson Barracks National Cemetery in St. Louis County, Missouri. She died on January 19, 1809.⁷

Alice's father, Robert Allen Forsyth or Forsythe, was also a veteran of the War of 1812. He married Margaret Lytle, and they had three children, the last named Alice Mariane Sophia. She was beautiful and vivacious, according to her daughter's recollections, and sought to remedy her "lack of school advantages early in life" through self-study even after becoming a mother. Eunice was both beautiful and bright and blessed with a vivid and accurate memory into her 80s.

In the last decade of life, Eunice Tripler moved to Grand Island, Nebraska, to stay with her daughter Eunice and son-in-law, a member of the clergy, Louis A. Arthur. Her recollections were so compelling that he "began, without her observation or knowledge, to take short-hand notes" and to write them "in full form within the hour," his "constant aim being to preserve her own forms of expression." He secured private publication of a slim volume in 1910, the introduction being written in May of that year.⁸ Eunice Hunt Tripler had passed away on March 28, age 87.⁹ Interment took place on Thursday,

---

5. Richard J. Wright ed., *The John Hunt Memoirs: Early Years of the Maumee Basin, 1812-1835* (Maumee: Maumee Valley Historical Society, n.d.), 1, 74 n.1-3. A color image of Thomas Hunt appears on page 9.
6. Id. 2; Dwight H. Kelton, *Annals of Fort Mackinac* (Detroit: Detroit Free Press Printing Co., 1887), 40, 82.
7. Edward G. Longacre, *The Man Behind the Guns: A Military Biography of General Henry J. Hunt, Commander Of Artillery, Army Of The Potomac* (Cambridge: Da Capo Press, 2003), 20-21. Brigadier-General Henry Jackson Hunt (1819-1889) was Eunice's cousin. The family line ran deep in Massachusetts: her great-grandfather John Hunt (1716-1777), his father Samuel Hunt (1684-1770), and his father Thomas Hunt Sr. (1648-1722) were all born there. The immigrant, Ephraim Hunt (1610-1687), born in England, married in Massachusetts in 1645.
8. Eunice Tripler, *Some Notes of her Personal Recollections* (New York: The Grafton Press, 1910), 9.
9. *Detroit Free Press*, Mar. 31, 1910, p. 12.

March 31, 1910, in Historic Elmwood Cemetery in Detroit, a final resting place fittingly in the city she had lived in for many decades, next to that of her nearly forgotten husband.

Because of these circumstances, circulation was limited, and the recorded words were not edited by their speaker and contain an unvarnished level of candor. Her accounts of General Scott, for example, are far from sympathetic due to his pomposity. Southern politicians who aided pension applications by her mother and herself are remembered positively. Most historians treat favorably a noted civilian Civil War organization; she does not, because it got out the knives for her husband.

The Triplers served their country faithfully and helped enable the "new birth of freedom" that the Civil War produced with the prohibition of slavery. Dr. Tripler put his life on the line for that cause. Mrs. Tripler, as an Army wife, provided the kind of support that only those who undertake such a sacrifice can fully understand but all Americans should highly value. During the winter of the first year of the war, she came to Washington, aided him in tackling his mountain of paperwork, and attended congressional sessions that could enable a rise in her husband's rank. All citizens should hold appreciation for the couple's devotion to the sustaining of American democracy.

These colorful recollections originate from the mind and memory of a woman of wide-ranging experience. They reveal aspects of the Civil War era through a gendered lens, one that is not often enjoyed in studies of the period. We are enabled to think about the national crisis and the experience of war in new ways.

Eunice's memoirs thus are well worthy of revival and explication. Detailed, accurate, and full of intimate insights, they bring to life the people and the experiences that populated the 1800s and helped shape the nation of the 21st century. As America continues to grapple with and work towards fulfilling the founding declaration that all persons are created equal, endowed with inalienable rights to life, liberty, and the pursuit of happiness, her example remains relevant and instructional. Though neither wife nor husband was born in Michigan, both made it their home. They both contributed to the great, sacrificial response by Michiganders that helped achieve triumph in the great internecine war.

A companion volume to this work is planned to tell more fully the story of the life and military career of Eunice's husband. The legacy of Charles S. Tripler has been either overlooked or submerged into that of his successor as chief medical officer of McClellan's army, Dr. Jonathan Letterman. Politics undermined Tripler's career and narrowed the ending contributions of his forty years in the military. The injustice he suffered no doubt contributed to the many heartbreaks that Eunice Hunt Tripler endured.

Editorial Note

The entirety of the original printed *Recollections* amounts to 184 numbered pages of content. Portions extraneous to the main Hunt/Tripler stories or to the Civil War are excluded from the current work. Headings derive from the original publication. The text follows the arrangement and order in the original. Short introductory comments begin each section.

Ellipses are inserted to reflect omitted content and to join passages within each heading. Spelling is as presented in the original text.

To make a distinction between the author's words and editorial insertions, the two sections are set in different font styles. All footnotes are new, designed to provide helpful and informative annotations. For each quoted section, a footnote at the end provides the associated page numbers in the original. The obituary concludes the content in the 1910 publication.

Ranks of officers are typically those up to and including the end of the Peninsula Campaign.

The 1910 publication contains an index; the current work has a new Index.

The author's name is sometimes abbreviated to EH or EHT for simplicity sake, as is her husband's to CST.

As can be seen from the sources provided, EHT's capacity for memory during the final decade of her life, as presumably taken down with accuracy by her son-in-law, conformed in almost all instances with the historical record. It is not too much to say that her recall of events, names, dates, and circumstances prove a keenly intelligent mind.

Any errors herein are the sole responsibility of the undersigned.

—Jack Dempsey, Editor

MEMOIRS OF EUNICE HUNT TRIPLER

I. Some Family History

We take up EH's life with a heroic anecdote about her ancestor, Thomas Hunt. None other than Alexander Hamilton, delegate to the Constitutional Convention, first U.S. Secretary of the Treasury, and subject of a 21st century hit Broadway musical, identified him as among the party of four hundred soldiers who played a key role in the victory at Yorktown, Virginia, in October 1781. The British position on their left flank was protected by two earthworks, Redoubts No. 9 and 10. French troops stormed the former; an American contingent under the command of Lieutenant-Colonel Hamilton was tasked with taking the latter. Her memoir commenced with the story:

In General Alexander Hamilton's account of the capture of the Yorktown redoubt ... he states that Thomas Hunt (my paternal Grand-Father) was wounded by a bayonet thrust. ... My Grand-Father reached the rank of Colonel some time after the war. He was in command of his regiment however, at the last assault at Yorktown.[1]
... My Grand-Father was one of the founders of the Society of the Cincinnati.[2]

---

1. *Recollections*, 13.
2. *Recollections*, 14. The Society was formed to perpetuate the relationships established during the American Revolution among officers. CST would become an original member of the Aztec Society, a comparable organization for veterans of the Mexican-American War, and of the Military Order of the Loyal Legion of the United States for Union officers who served in the Civil War.

That recollection was quite accurate:

★ ★ ★

Camp Before York Town, Oct. 15, 1781
Sir:
I have the honor to render you an account of the corps under my command in your attack of last night upon the redoubt on the left of the enemy's lines. ...

Captain Bets, of Laurens's corps, Captain Hunt and Lieutenant Mansfield, of Gimat's, were wounded with the bayonet in gallantly entering the work.

Major-General the Marquis De La Fayette.[3]

★ ★ ★

The military record and courage exhibited by her father's father at a crucial moment of the nation's founding provided EH with a proud legacy, which she would not forsake during either her single or married life. So, too, on her mother's side:

My maternal Grand-Father, Robert Forsythe, was agent for the Astors in the fur trade in Detroit (The North Western Fur Co.). ... My Grand-Father became an officer in the War of 1812, and is referred to by Mrs. Emma Willard in her history, "The Republic of America" as "that brave partisan officer Forsythe." He died while on the journey to his home in Detroit after the close of the war. His widow made her home in Amherstburg, Canada. The children were three: Robert, Maria (Kercheval), and Alice (Hunt).[4]

Again, EH's memory proves accurate. In chapter VIII of the work cited, dealing with the "Campaign of 1813," is found this account:

---

3. John C. Hamilton ed., *The Works of Alexander Hamilton; Comprising His Correspondence, and His Political and Official Writings*, Vol. I (New York: John F. Trow, 1851), 270-272.
4. *Recollections*, 14.

Early in February, Major Forsyth, an enterprising partisan officer, who commanded some American troops stationed at Ogdensburg, crossed the St. Lawrence with a party of his riflemen and some volunteers, surprised the guard at Elizabethtown , and took fifty-two prisoners, together with a quantity of arms and ammunition.[5]

My parents, Thomas Hunt and Alice Forsythe, were married in Detroit, 29 September, 1821, by a Judge Abbott. At the time there was no Protestant Minister in the place. My Father was born in Watertown, Mass., in 1794. His Father (Thos. Hunt) being in the Army received orders to go to Detroit. The family accompanied him when my Father was a little boy. Thence my Grand-Father was ordered to Fort Wayne (now in Indiana). The trip was made by batteaux[6] propelled by oars, through the Detroit River, Lake Erie and the Maumee River. Camp was made every night on the bank. But the family was large and burdensome and it was almost impossible to make the journey with all the necessities that had to be carried. The eldest brother of my Father (Henry I.) had already gone into business in Detroit and had established an extensive trade with the Indians there.[7] On the Fort Wayne journey it was therefore decided to send back my Uncle George and my Father to their Brother in Detroit. On their arrival they found the town had meantime been burned down and a more desolate scene could not be imagined. There was no one to receive them. The boys sat down on the river bank with their arms around each other's necks and cried. The eldest brother was soon found, however, and the younger

---

5. Emma Willard, *History of the United States, or, Republic of America* (New York: A.S. Barnes & Co., 1845), 323.
6. A long, light, flat-bottom boat.
7. Henry Jackson Hunt (1786-1826) served as second Mayor of Detroit and was among the "prominent citizens" of early Detroit. Silas Farmer, *The History of Detroit and Michigan or The Metropolis Illustrated* (Detroit: Silas Farmer & Co., 1889), 48. As a merchant, "he occupied a high rank" whose death caused universal regret. Charles Lanman, *The Red Book of Michigan; A Civil, Military and Biographical History* (Detroit: E.B. Smith & Co., 1871), 450.

boys became associated with him in his business. When the War of 1812 broke out, my Father, then seventeen, received an appointment as Lieutenant. He needed to be mounted and borrowed a white horse of his Brother, Henry I. Hunt.[8] He was in the battle of Brownstown below Detroit.[9] ... After Hull's surrender, the detachment to which my Father belonged, not knowing that event, marched to Detroit. The flag was down on the Fort, but, before they could comprehend the situation, the British forces surrounded and took them.[10] And almost immediately began the prisoners' long march to Montreal. A companion of my Father on this journey was Col. Snelling for whom Fort Snelling was named[11], being the first Commandant of the post, and who but three days before had been married to my Father's sister, Abbie. She, too, accompanied her husband, a cart being provided for the two or three women who were so taken. Of this fearful journey, over 550 miles, made entirely afoot, my Father scarcely ever spoke in later years. I remember, however, his saying that the soldiers suffered dreadfully from dysentery but that those who ate most freely of ripe peaches as they passed certain orchards, made best recovery.[12] ...

As a result of his Montreal captivity, my Father contracted rheumatism and a white swelling in the right knee. Finally the officers were exchanged and returned to the United States. My Father and Col. Snelling came to Boston and there my Father had a terrible illness. After a time Col. Snelling had to part from my Father for duty

---

8. After the Battle of Gettysburg, Eunice's cousin Henry wrote her about horseshoe nails that "wouldn't hold a shoe for two days" and had frustrated the pursuit of the Rebel army. *Minneapolis Star*, Sept. 20, 1933, p. 4 (reporting on donation of the letter by a Hunt/Tripler descendant).
9. *Recollections*, 16-17. The fire that destroyed Detroit occurred on June 11, 1805, after which the "Woodward Plan" proposed a redesign of the town. The battle occurred on August 5, 1812.
10. *Recollections*, 18. On August 16, 1812, General William Hull surrendered Fort Detroit to the British and their indigenous allies.
11. Josiah Snelling (1782-1828) was the inaugural commander of this fort in Minnesota. Abby S. Chaplin, his wife, was Thomas Hunt's sister. She received a widow's pension.
12. *Recollections*, 17-18.

elsewhere but he left money to defray the expenses of my Father's burial, fully believing he would die. My Father, however, recovered and returned to Detroit. The army was soon reorganized. It was a good opportunity to squeeze out undesirable officers but my Father was retained.[13] ...

My Uncle, Robert Forsythe, had become Private Secretary to Gen. Cass[14] in Detroit. His Mother was living in Amherstburg. Gen. Cass told him he ought to bring up his sisters to Detroit. This he did and my Mother and her sister boarded with a Mrs. Roby and went to school. There my Father met her and they were married when he was twenty-seven and she seventeen. Already her elder sister, Maria, had married and, as Mrs. Kercheval, was living at Fort Wayne, Indiana.[15] ... My Uncle Forsythe bought in New York for my Mother's wedding outfit a handsome lilac dress, a large white Leghorn hat[16] and lace cape. These she wore when married. My Father's Regiment was soon ordered to Prairie du Chien[17] but he was really no longer fit for active duty, young as he was. And there was no retired list in those days. So he was ordered to Washington for duty in the Commissary General's office. This was the wedding trip. They went to Buffalo on the Steamer "Walk-in-the-Water" accounted a very fine vessel and the first steamer on the lakes.[18] ...

My Mother always felt the lack of school advantages in early life—or there were no such in Amherstburg. She studied very hard while she had the opportunity in Detroit—and she even continued her studies after her first child was born. Her manners were quiet and dignified and she had great tact. She was thought in Washington to be a remarkable representative of Michigan, that "land of wild Indians." She used to say that she learned very much from Scott's Novels which

---

13. *Recollections*, 19.
14. Lewis Cass (1782-1866), Governor of the Michigan Territory at this time.
15. *Recollections*, 20. Kercheval is a major avenue on the east side of Detroit.
16. A wide-brimmed and flat-topped hat made of straw.
17. In Wisconsin.
18. *Recollections*, 21.

appeared during her early married life. I remember my Mother, when I was a child, often keeping a spelling-book under her pillow.[19]

II. Washington in Early Days

In this section, EH recalls a small town that served as the capital of a still new nation – small enough for the famous to be next-door neighbors. She recounts experiences with many. It was also a Southern town in which slavery had always been lawful.

For six or eight months after their arrival in Washington my Parents boarded and then began house-keeping. Their move was in all ways a pleasant one. My Father was very gentle and winning and my Mother had much beauty and a most engaging manner and their friends were many. The Army circle itself was delightful. I was born 11 October, 1822, and I had a very happy childhood. My Mother was ambitious for me and wanted me only with children who were refined. My clothes were always right and I never had mortification on that ground. The care of us children rested on our darky Nurse, "Mammie Nellie."[20] She was devoted to our family and took the greatest pride in our affairs. It was the custom to give household servants a dress at Christmas and again on their birthday, and turbans and kerchiefs were frequent presents. So our Nellie could save nearly all her earnings and was quite independent when we left the city. Such devoted service I greatly missed in the new order of the household when we came to Detroit. I was named after my Father's Mother, "Eunice Wellington" but at my Baptism, after my marriage, I dropped the second name.[21]
…

---

19. *Recollections*, 22-23. Walter Scott was a Scottish novelist, author of such works of fiction as *Ivanhoe*, *The Lady of the Lake*, and *Rob Roy*.
20. The word "darky" was an alternative spelling of terms referring to "dark-skinned person" and a reflection of the racial attitudes prevalent in a city where, until 1862, slavery was lawful.
21. *Recollections*, 25-26.

We had four servants in our Washington home. These were all slaves and their wages were paid of course to their owners who in turn had but to furnish their clothing. We liked this arrangement because, if they misconducted, we could report them and, at once, get rid of them. My Father used to say "Never mind what we think of slavery. These are our friends about us and we are grateful to them for a thousand favours. We must not denounce what we may happen to question."[22] ...

My most intimate playmates were the daughters of General Alexander McComb and the daughter of General Cass.[23] ...

My only pets were birds. I had a beautiful Cardinal bird which Purser Watson of the Navy brought me from South America, a Mocking-bird and a pair of Canaries. Of all these I became very fond.

When I was a very young infant, I was vaccinated at three separate points on my arm, about one and one half inches apart, as was the custom of the time. Many persons regarded small-pox in the spirit of fatalism and, as though it were wrong to withstand so direct a visitation of God. Still it was so common a scourge there was universal fear of it and inoculation for the disease itself was by no means rare – for this was believed to induce a milder type of the malady. Travel by stage-coach was thought to expose one specially – but, in truth, people did not know and then, as now, ignorance begot talk – and I well remember the long and earnest wranglings on the subject.

The Church seemed dead in Washington. Parson Hawley (always called "Captain" Hawley on account of his army service) was the Rector of St. John's Church which we attended. He always wore a wig

---

22. *Recollections*, 26. EH would later condemn cruelty to the enslaved by their oppressors. Id. 44-45; 126. In 1820, the number of enslaved persons only slightly outnumbered "Free blacks," 1,945-1,796. Constance M. Green, *The Secret City: A History of Race Relations in the Nation's Capital* (Princeton: Princeton University Press, 1967), 33.
23. *Recollections*, 26. Major-General Alexander Macomb (1782-1841) served as Commanding General of the U.S. Army from 1828 to 1841. He and wife Catherine had three daughters. Lewis and Elizabeth Cass had five daughters, one of whom, Matilda, is mentioned.

and small clothes and a Clerk made the responses in service. Captain Hawley preached, of course, not in the surplice but in the black gown, which was the universal custom of my childhood, the change from surplice to gown being made just before the commencement of the sermon. The organ was above and behind the pulpit which latter was the old-fashioned three-decker. Directly back of the pulpit (but beneath the organ) was the shelf which served as the Communion Table. My Father, on account of his lameness, always stood through the prayers for he could not kneel and would not sit. A Mr. Goldsborough, the Father of two Admirals of our Navy, used to dilate on the beauty of the service but I was hardly so impressed as I might have been.[24] ...

President Jackson[25] attended St. John's. I used often to see him walking to and fro in front of the White House sunning himself. I remember one day when I was wearing a sun-bonnet President Jackson stopped me on the walk in front of the White House and patted my head and asked me if I went to Mr. Haskell's school. He knew all the local institutions. I remember his white hair brushed straight up from his forehead – and how his long legs seemed to span the sidewalk. His countenance by most people was thought hard and repellant – but he was very friendly and benevolent to us children. I always felt I had a side-walk acquaintance with him.

The demonstration on each 8th January (New Orleans)[26] was something a child could never forget – the firing of guns in the morning, later a parade of the marines and other organizations, the formal calling on Pres. Jackson by all the officers in Washington, (my Father, of course, in full uniform with sword and plumed chapeau), and, lastly, a grand ball in the evening.

---

24. *Recollections*, 28-29. Smallpox would be a recurring challenge for EH's husband. St. John's Episcopal Church is located at Sixteenth Street and H Street N.W. on Lafayette Square and dates from 1816. The Greek Revival structure was designed by Benjamin Latrobe, first architect of the U.S. Capitol.
25. Andrew Jackson (1767-1845), 7th U.S. president, who, in the nullification crisis of 1832–33, stood for Federal supremacy over State's rights.
26. Commemorating Jackson's victory as commanding general in the victory at the Battle of New Orleans in 1815.

There were but four departments in the general administration of the Government, State, Treasury, War and Navy. These departments occupied four separate buildings at the corners of the square in the centre of which stood and still stands the White House. We children would ramble through the halls of the War Department Building for its refreshing coolness. My Father was on duty, as Captain, in the Commissary General's office of the War Department. The army numbered but 8,000 men and there was little to do. There were three clerks only with my Father in his room. Gen. Gibson was Commissary General. The father of Gen. E.O.C. Ord was a messenger in this department.[27] ...

At about the age of four years I saw Gen. Lafayette[28] many times. He was a stupid-looking man with high shoulders. He used to take me on his lap and talk to me about his little Grand-daughter in France. I remember wearing a little pair of yellow kid shoes with an outline picture of Lafayette stamped on the toe. Everything then bore his picture. I remember showing my shoes to Lafayette and they amused him much. The meeting with him came about thus. Gen. Bernard[29] of our Army was an intimate friend of Lafayette and lived just around the corner from our house. While in Washington Lafayette stayed at his home. He was a Frenchman by birth, at the head of the Engineer Corps and had come to this country at the time of the American Revolution under the influence of Lafayette and remained here. My Father called on Lafayette, well knowing the service his own Father had had with Lafayette at Yorktown during the Revolution and Lafayette used, then, to come to our house. He used to walk round the corner

---

27. *Recollections*, 30-32. Contemporary maps show the War Department Building at the northeast corner of Pennsylvania Avenue and Seventeenth Street. Edward Otho Cresap Ord (1818-1883), West Point Class of 1839, served in the Seminole conflicts and as Union Major-General in the Civil War.
28. The Marquis de La Fayette (1757-1834), commissioned by the Continental Congress as Major-General in 1777.
29. Likely, Simon Bernard (1779-1839), émigré to America, commissioned as an engineer in 1816. He worked on designs for Fort Monroe, Virginia, and Fort Morgan, Alabama, both strategic points during the Civil War.

from Gen. Bernard's house to our home and sit with my Father on the small front portico and tell him funny experiences and escapades of my Grand Father in the Yorktown Campaign. I am exceedingly sorry I have never known just what these were. Lafayette would send Sophie Bernard round to our house to get me and then he would pet me and give me sweets and nuts such as no child of four or five years ought ever to have. My Father was the envy of the neighborhood from these attentions of the great man of the day.[30] ...

Our house was on the corner of F St. and 17th.[31] When coming from Pennsylvania Avenue we would pass by the South side of the White House for shortness. When I went East in 1856 to meet Dr. Tripler[32] on his return from California, I found the site of our house, but much was changed. F St. itself was being then cut down and graded at that point and all was confusion. I found, however, just round the corner the place where, as a child, I used to buy gingerbread "horse-cakes."[33] I had gone to that shop hand in hand with Lafayette when only three or four years old – and remembered it well. I was not permitted to forget it. There can be but few persons now living in this country who touched Lafayette, and whom he kissed.[34] ...

My Father always kept a horse, one of his army allowances being

---

30. *Recollections*, 33-34. Lafayette was in Washington from October 12-17, November 22 and in early December, 1824, then in January-February (departing on the 22nd) and again before final departure on September 7, 1825. Auguste Levasseur, *Lafayette in America, in 1824 and 1825*, Vol. I (Philadelphia: Carey & Lea, 1829), 167, 174, 227; Vol. II, 9, 30, 241, 248-249. Bernard is mentioned several times.

31. The intersection is today bounded by the Eisenhower Executive Office Building and the Winder Building, which dates from 1848 – no other structures remain here from EH's youth. Around the corner on 18th Street, however, the "Octagon House" dates from 1799. In the Lafayette Square Historic District to the northeast, six period structures she knew still remain: Blair House; Cutts-Madison House; Decatur House; St. John's Church, and Parish House; and Tayloe-Cameron House.

32. Though EH typically referred to him this way, in their day-to-day intimate communications she called him "Charlie." *Recollections*, 135.

33. A horse-cake was a gingerbread cookie shaped like the animal.

34. *Recollections*, 34-35.

for its feed. By this horse, "Rhoderick" by name, I came near my death when about four years old. I was upon his back when he suddenly bolted away from the servant and into the stable—and I had a narrow escape from being crushed.

My Mother used to take me to hear great debates in Congress, but all that interested me was the sight of the crowds. My Father, Henry Clay and Daniel Webster were all members of the same card club and met weekly. But my Father did not remain long an active member – because the play was too high for him. Gen. Gratiot we knew intimately. I was often with the daughters of Lewis Maclean and at their house I met Washington Irving repeatedly. I remember his coming into the room suddenly where we were playing "Hide and Seek" and my fear lest he should sit down on the divan under which I was hid. The Maclean girls used to stick pins in his favorite chair. Lydia Maclean married Gen. Joe Johnston. I remember Martin Van Buren well. At this time he was in Jackson's cabinet. His son, "Prince John" as he was called, went abroad and was most favorably received by the young Queen Victoria. I recall Martin Van Buren's foxy red hair brushed straight out from the sides. I remember going once with a party to the "Great Falls" of the Potomac above the city – and being much impressed by them.[35] ...

The Woodbury mansion on Lafayette Square I knew well. Levi Woodbury was Secretary of War in Jackson's Cabinet. There were

---

35. *Recollections*, 35-36. Henry Clay (1777-1852) was known as the "Great Compromiser," responsible for the Compromise of 1850 that averted potential civil war. Daniel Webster (1782-1852), famed orator, uttered "Liberty and Union, now and for ever, one and inseparable!" on the floor of the U.S. Senate. Charles Chouteau Gratiot (1786-1855) served in the War of 1812. Louis McLane (1786-1857) was another veteran of the War of 1812; he served in various appointed and elected Federal positions. His daughter, Lydia Mulligan Sims McLane (1822-1887), married Joseph E. Johnston (1807-1891), West Point Class of 1829, who became perhaps a leading General in the Confederate military during the Civil War. Washington Irving (1783-1859) was a famous American author. Martin Van Buren (1782-1862) was 8th President of the United States. Various accounts report that John Van Buren (1810-1866) attended the Coronation of Queen Victoria.

three daughters – and it was the second of these, Frank or Frances, I knew best, being her class-mate in school. Her elder sister, Lizzie, married Montgomery Blair, Lincoln's first Postmaster General.[36] With her I renewed my acquaintance in the Winter of 1861-'62 while I was in Washington with my husband.

The two daughters of Chief Justice Taney[37] I remember seeing at our house and hearing them talk of certain beaux and their attentions. I have no memory of their father. The home of the Taneys was on the street fronting the White House, corresponding in location to the house of Secretary Levi Woodbury.[38] …

I knew Gen. Jacob Brown, Commanding General of the Army. I was intimate with his daughter Kate, and often at their house, where my Mother, too, frequently visited. I have a vivid memory of the General, tall, thin and of dark complexion. On the death of Gen. Brown (no retirement for age in those days) Gen. Alexander McComb succeeded to the post. His daughter Jane, three weeks older than I, was my class-mate and play-mate, as was also Matilda Cass. Of course I was often at Gen. McComb's. He was a *bon vivant*, very gross-looking and loaded with fat. His second wife brought him much wealth and, the first thing after marrying him, paid up his old debts. Gen. McComb was succeeded by Gen. Winfield Scott.[39] …

---

36.   Montgomery Blair (1813-1883), Postmaster-General from 1861-1864.
37.   Roger B. Taney (1777-1864), 5th Chief Justice of the U.S., author of the *Dred Scott* decision in 1857.
38.   *Recollections*, 38.
39.   *Recollections*, 39-40. Jacob Brown (1775-1828) was appointed Commanding General of the U.S. Army in 1821 and held the position until his death. Alexander Macomb succeeded Brown and served until Winfield Scott (1786-1866) was appointed. Matilda Frances Cass (1818–1898) was a daughter of Lewis Cass; she married Henry Ledyard (1812-1880), Mayor of Detroit in 1855. The Macomb house was at the northwest corner of 17th and I Streets NW, just a few blocks due north. Hal H. Smith, "Historic Washington Homes" in *Records of the Columbia Historical Society, Washington, D.C.*, Vol. 11 (1908), 243, 262. Other period structures still exist that EH would have known, such as the colonial home at 2017 I Street NW. Maud Burr Morris, *An Old Washington Mansion* (reprint from *Records of the Columbia Historical Society, Washington, D.C.*, vol. 21, 1918).

Elderly women generally wore black silk skirts and a kerchief crossed over the breast. Often there was an astonishing turban for a head covering and frequently black mitts on the hands. A slit cut in the skirt admitted the hand to a pocket, which was tied on as a bag below. In this there were a red silk handkerchief and a white one for display, a silver snuff box and a small nutmeg grater. By the use of this last each woman could determine the amount of spice in her sangaree (a drink of wine, water and sugar) or her negus (a hot drink). I was often disgusted by all this.

I think it was not till after our going to Detroit in 1836 that I first saw granulated sugar.[40] ...

Our friends in Washington were as intelligent, as cultivated and as refined as any circle to be found anywhere in the country at the time. Yet social custom was such that I early learned as a child to get out of the way of certain men who visited at our house. I could not bear to be caressed and kissed by men who were intoxicated and I would not stand it. Many of my Parents' neighbors and intimate friends had slaves as domestic servants and therefore no wages to pay. So far as table manners and etiquette are concerned I feel quite sure that the ordinary observances of the time when I was a child were better than customs now. One seldom or never saw a household which was lacking a sufficient number of servants, and these servants were all trained. The children, too, were sure to be quiet and mannerly. The table service and furnishing were perhaps not quite so elaborate as what one may see to-day, but all articles were better cared for. Table forks had but two prongs and it was quite impossible to use them for eating peas. Knives and forks, too, had almost universally handles of horn and these often were silver mounted, but they would be skewy and unlike others of the set. Ivory handles came into use later but, almost invariably, the ivory became checked and cracked.[41]

---

40. *Recollections*, 42. First Lady Dolley Todd Madison (1768-1849) was well-known for wearing a turban. Michigan did not become a State in the Union until 1837.
41. The social scene in Washington during the late 1820s-1830s reflected a

In the painting in the rotunda of the Capitol, the "Baptism of Pocahontas" (now reproduced on the back of the $20 green-backs), I was taken as the model of a page. In my Father's office one day the artist (I think his name was Chapman) said he wanted my head. My Father laughed and said, "Only on Saturdays." So every Saturday for a number of weeks I came to the office to sit for him. The likeness was apparent to all my friends when the painting was completed. This was about 1832. The figure for which I sat is in the left foreground of the picture.[42] ...

The house directly opposite our Washington home was occupied by the family of a Mr. Houston, who was a brother of Sam Houston, the Governor of Texas. This Mr. Houston was much at our house and always talking of his brother Sam.[43]

Gen. Towson (who served in the war of 1812) lived just opposite the Navy Department – and the home of most of the cabinet officers and the principal foreign ministers fronted on Lafayette Square. Next to our house and on the corner of F Street lived Gen. Gratiot. Directly opposite upon the corner lived Gen. Alexander Ramsey, Secretary of War – and opposite him, but diagonally opposite Gen. Gratiot's, was the home of the Pleasantons, but a half square from our house. Clementina Pleasanton, her sister and I used to play in the front yard of the Pleasanton home, lock arms and walk up and down in our deep sun-bonnets which I hated. I remember seeing Martin Van Buren enter this house for a call, while we girls commented on his bald head and stiffly growing whiskers. James Buchanan was also an intimate friend of the Pleasantons. I remember well his portly figure and how

---

rather small circle. See, e.g., Margaret Bayard Smith, *The First Forty Years of Washington Society*, Gaillard Hunt ed. (New York: Charles Scribner's Sons, 1906), 238-242.

42. *Recollections*, 47-48. The 12' by 18' oil painting, completed by John Gadsby Chapman (1808-1889) in 1840, remains hanging in the Rotunda of the U.S. Capitol. A cholera epidemic swept through Washington in 1832, but EH did not mention and apparently did not contract it. J.D. Dickey, *Empire of Mud: The Secret History of Washington, DC* (Guilford: Lyons Press, 2014), 104.

43. *Recollections*, 48-49.

he would often stop to speak to us girls and to stroke my head. I can just remember once seeing John Quincy Adams when I was very young. He was, however, at a distance when pointed out to me as the President. I never met him in person.[44]

Martin Van Buren was quite undersized as a man. It would have been an impossible thing for him ever to have assumed any nobility of bearing. His sons John and Abram were often at our house, the latter the more frequently, as he belonged to a certain card club which met weekly at the houses of the members. He used to borrow and wear a certain uniform suit of my Father's for evening companies, and when at last my Father resigned from the army and was about to move to Detroit Abram Van Buren came to my Father to ask if he could buy the uniform. Of course my Father was very glad to sell it to him. At this time Martin Van Buren was in Jackson's cabinet.[45]

The Cass home was on G. St. immediately in the rear of our house. An opening was made in the fence so that we could pass backward and forward, and the families were very intimate. Of course Mrs. Cass had known my Mother in Detroit. In her own early home in Virginia there were shoals of slaves, and it was a change indeed when she came as a young wife to Detroit, where she had as servant only one young Indian. Mrs. Cass was such an invalid that she could take no social duty. During their first Winter in Washington, therefore, Gen. Cass sent for the wife of Gen. John E. Wool of Troy, N.Y., to come to Washington and matronize his three daughters. As the

---

44. *Recollections*, 49. Nathaniel Towson (1784-1854) attained the rank of Brevet Major-General in the Army. Alexander Ramsey (1815-1903) was Secretary of War in 1879-1881. Clementina (1830-1888) and Laura Pleasanton (died 1893, age 78) were younger sisters of two Civil War Generals, Augustus James Pleasanton (1808-1894) and Alfred Pleasanton (1824-1897), commander of the Cavalry Corps of the Army of the Potomac. Their father was Stephen Pleasanton (1776-1855), reputed to have helped save the Declaration of Independence and other historical documents from the British during their attack on Washington in 1814. John Quincy Adams (1767-1848) was 6th President of the United States.
45. *Recollections*, 50. Van Buren served as Secretary of State in 1829-1831. Abraham Van Buren II (1807-1873) was his eldest son.

second Winter approached, he was asked if the arrangement would be repeated. "'No,'" he replied, "Mrs. Hunt will succeed to that post." And my Mother did this with tact and great credit to herself.[46]

My Mother had a beautiful figure and a strikingly handsome face. She was vivacious and a fine dancer and, naturally, was in great demand at all festivities. On one occasion Sir Charles Vaughn[47] gave a large entertainment in honour of certain English visitors in Washington. An invitation was sent to my Mother but none to my Father. My Mother promptly sent a polite declination. This brought Sir Charles himself to our house to importune my Mother. He said to her, "Mrs. Hunt, I wish especially to show our American beauties to our English friends." "But," said my Mother, "my husband, Capt. Hunt, is not invited." "Oh, Hunt," said Sir Charles, "Oh, damn Hunt." My Mother said no word, but rose and stood perfectly erect before him. It was her house and he, of course, saw the interview had ended and took his departure.

In my childhood the Capitol was completed, but not the wings as now. There was a field with rank, coarse grass on the North side of the White House. Not long before we left, Pennsylvania Avenue was macadamized, but the sides were rough and made horrible walking, a central rut only having been worn smooth by vehicles. There was a double row of Lombardy poplars on this avenue from the White House to the Capitol. Some evergreens and a few deciduous trees had been planted in the White House grounds – but all seemed untrimmed and uncared for.[48] …

The school I attended was next to St. John's Church. I remember very well the coarsely printed little blue covered primer out of which

---

46. *Recollections*, 50-51. Elizabeth Spencer Cass (1786-1853) descended from a General in the Continental Army. John Ellis Wool (1784-1869) served in the War of 1812, the Mexican-American War, and the Civil War. "Shoals" refers to a large number.
47. Charles Richard Vaughan (1774-1849) was a British diplomat in Washington from 1825-1835. Sidney Lee ed., *Dictionary of National Biography*, Vol. LVIII (New York: Macmillan Co., 1899), 161.
48. *Recollections*, 51-52. The wings to the Capitol were added in the 1850s.

I learned my letters. The syllables, ba, be, bi, bo, bu, and ca, ce, ci, co, cu, and so on down through the alphabet, were arranged in columns. There were a few wretchedly drawn, grotesque woodcuts by way of illustration. The profiles of men and boys were ludicrously awry. There is hardly a school boy to-day who could not do better with his pencil. Apples on a tree would be about the size of pumpkins, and a boy would be as tall as the tree. The pasteboard cover of this primer was so coarse that pieces of the cloth out of which it was made were quite visible.[49] …

I was made quite a pet by my French teacher and got a good start in the language very early. A Mr. Eugene Vaile who was connected with the French Embassy kept house with two sisters in the "Seven Buildings" on Pennsylvania Avenue and they would come and get me and talk French with me and then take me to my Mother that she might hear what I had just been taught. This all encouraged me and made me like the language too. At this time I was about six years old. The Cass family had brought from France a great quantity of French books—and of all these I had the use later. The Cass daughters all spoke French and I was much with them. When out of other reading-matter, how often have I gotten a French play or novel from the Cass library!—I have read current French literature with ease and delight since I was eleven years old.[50] …

In the Washington I knew as a child there were no street cars, no public schools, no pavements, no public sewers, no friction matches, no telegraphs, telephones, daguerreotypes nor photographs, no cheap postage, no city water and scarcely any street lamps. A little attempt was made to light the chief thoroughfares with oil lamps at certain corners. All ordinary lamps smelled horribly. In the theatres this nuisance was overpowering. But people seemed to throng the theatres. I was taken, for example, young as I then was, to see Fanny Kemble play

---

49. *Recollections*, 52.
50. *Recollections*, 54-55. The library reference is suggestive of visits by EH to the Cass family home on West Fort Street.

Juliet to her Father's Romeo.[51] I saw Joseph Jefferson (the Father of the creator of "Rip-Van- Winkle") as Dogberry.[52] It was quite customary for the audience to eat oranges during the performance and throw the peel anywhere on the floor. I often went to horse-races. My Mother and everyone would bet gloves or anything that struck their fancy. The question of propriety was never raised. The foreign element, the French especially, were very determinate of social forms in Washington. My parents played cards frequently and for money. Everybody did so then. The game was "Loo" and the counters were pieces of mother-of-pearl and in form of a fish—rather handsome toys in themselves.[53] People bet on anything and everything—on whether it would rain to-morrow or the next day—on whether Jack would win his present bet or whether Jim would lose. Gamblers often came from other cities bringing new tricks and simply proving themselves robbers.

Child as I was, I instinctively felt this gambling was all wrong. I have seen my Father grow pale on comparing notes with my Mother, at learning they both had lost, at different tables.

I remember I went to a circus once and, with some other children, had a ride in a howdah on an elephant.[54] I can recall now vividly our sensations from the movements of the great beast. I remember seeing a play in Ford's Theatre long afterward the scene of the awful tragedy of Lincoln's assassination. As I recall it, it was not a very large place of entertainment.

There was always the greatest respect shown to age and deference to those in high office – very different from customs now. Washington life, as I recall it, was quite aristocratic and showed a marked tendency

---

51. Frances Anne Kemble was a noted British actress and eldest daughter of actor Charles Kemble. In 1832, the two undertook a theatrical tour of the United States.
52. Joseph Jefferson Jr. was an actor, as was his son, Joseph Jefferson III; the latter constructed a home in 1870 on an island near New Iberia, Louisiana, that still today is known as Rip Van Winkle Gardens. Dogberry refers to a character in William Shakespeare's *Much Ado About Nothing*.
53. Loo, or Lanterloo, was a popular card game.
54. A howdah is a seat.

toward class distinction. It was a real shock to me, after our move to Detroit, to see young women engage in general conversation with shop clerks over the counter.[55] ...

There was a good market near our house and a servant, a free colored man, always attended my Father with a basket to bring home his purchases. This servant, when we left Washington, went to Gen. Cass and Mrs. Cass pronounced him the best servant they ever had.

My Father was of a rather delicate physique. His fearful experiences in 1814 had permanently impaired his health. I can see my Mother now meeting him at the gate when he reached home in Summer from the office, white with exhaustion and heat, and refreshing him with a drink of cold whiskey and water.[56] ...

One of our visitors in Washington was my Cousin, John Kinzie, of Fort Dearborn or Chicago—after whom "Kinzie" Street in that city is named. He came to Washington with a certain delegation of Indians who desired to see the "Great Father" for redress of their wrongs. Cheating the poor Indian was a common thing. But John Kinzie was an honest man and known as the Red Man's Friend. As a young man he had spent much time visiting and hunting with the Pottawattamie Indians—having a liking for their wild life and finding he made friends by it. I remember well how he entertained us children with an Indian dance which was meant to depict the treatment an Indian gives to his enemies—noiselessly stealing round in a circle—lifting his feet till his heels actually touched his thighs—peering cautiously about on every side for his foe—at last spying his enemy, leaping upon him and bearing him to the ground. Later, in our home in Detroit, he and Uncle Forsythe used to talk together in the Indian tongue, having much in sympathy from their common Indian experiences.

With a little circle of my Washington mates I had instruction in sewing. Our teacher once told us that we should always take three more stitches after the needleful of thread had become so short as to

---

55. *Recollections*, 56-58.
56. *Recollections*, 58-59.

make it necessary to re-thread the needle at each stitch. All this for economy's sake but I doubt if it were really expected we would carry out the direction.

When the Railway was completed from Washington to Baltimore, my Father took me for the day to the latter city.[57] It was thought to be a marvel of achievement that this journey could be made in two hours. We returned in the evening with a fine shawl which we purchased in Baltimore as a present for my Mother.

While Andrew Jackson was making new deposits of the public funds, my Father accepted the office of messenger and carried the sum of $60,000 to Little Rock, Arkansas. It was difficult to find trusty men for the service because of the great peril incurred, but my Father took the duty for the sake of the additional pay. I remember my Father bringing the big bundle home, taking it up stairs and spreading out the packages of bills on the bed where my Mother proceeded at once to take the necessary measurements and quilt the money into a wide belt he wore. When she had finished her task she had a fit of hysterics. My Father was appointed to this extraordinary service perhaps for his known soldierly character—and, it may perhaps have been felt, that his lameness would have a tendency to disarm suspicion. My Father used to say that he had often been in posts of danger but never, as he felt, in greater peril than on this journey. Arkansas and the whole South West region at this time were infested with ruffians willing to murder any man for five dollars.

Fanny Bell, daughter of Senator John Bell of Tennessee, candidate for the Presidency in 1860, passed the Christmas Holidays, one year, at our house. She was attending a boarding-school in Washington at the time. She sent me a gold ring shortly afterward – the first ring I ever possessed.[58]

My Brother "Bob," when a small boy, was one day trundling a little

---

57. The Baltimore & Ohio Railroad opened the line in August 1835.
58. *Recollections*, 59-61. Frances Fanny Bell (1820-1847) was one of five children of John Bell (1796-1869), the Constitutional Union Party candidate in 1860, and Sally Dickinson (1802-1832).

wheelbarrow along Pennsylvania Avenue. His head was down and he was running at top speed when he ran his barrow right between the legs of President Jackson himself. It was a funny sight, so bystanders said, to see the President gather himself together and slowly lift one long leg over the boy's head.

I felt I knew every brick-bat in Washington and loved it, and, when we left, it was with tears and groans on my part.[59]

III. Detroit in Early Days

This section begins with the financial reasons for the move back to Detroit. Her father resigned from the Army to accept a post as Register of the Land Office, made possible by President Jackson's appointment on the recommendation of Secretary of State Cass.[60] The text evolves into a lengthy portrayal, nearly all unsympathetic, of the indigenous peoples that interacted with her family as well as people of European descent as the Hunts made their way to Michigan.

When we made our journey to the West we were three days on the Hudson River from New York to Albany. From Albany we went by canal to Oswego where we took [a] boat through the lakes. On our arrival in Detroit we spent six weeks at my Aunt Kercheval's. While there I met the English novelist Marryat. ... We were a party of five girls – my three Kercheval cousins, my Sister Ellen and myself. ... When we came to Detroit to live I felt soon reconciled to the change and thoroughly at home for it was quickly borne in on me that both my Father's family and my Mother's family had been largely instrumental in settling and developing the region.

Our first Detroit home was at the southeast corner of Congress and Shelby Streets.[61] Detroit, had at this time, had perhaps 8,000 pop-

---

59. *Recollections*, 62. Knowing "every brick-bat" means familiarity with every inch of every half-length of a customary brick.
60. He was only the fifth to hold the office. Farmer, 38.
61. Location of the Murphy-Telegraph Building.

ulation …. Jefferson Avenue was the principal street for retail shops. Woodward Avenue had the large churches, St. Paul's, the Presbyterian and the Methodist all being between Congress and Larned Streets. Bishop McCoskry and we came the same week in August, 1836. He became rector of St. Paul's. There was a swamp where the Grand Circus Park now is and the State Capitol (afterward burned) stood where later the High School was erected. On the Campus Martius the Michigan Central Railway soon after had it's [sic] station and sheds for cattle and freight. … We found much social life in Detroit. I knew every body.[62] … There were no yachts on the river and few small boats for pleasure. Every one had a cart for summer and a cutter for winter. Uncle Forsythe had a very fine sleigh. I was in demand for many tableaux. … There was no Fort Wayne as yet – but some artillery officers were stationed in the city.[63]

For a time I attended the school which stood where now is the City Hall. The principal was a Mr. Wilson who was the author of some books on mathematics. Some of the boys from Mr. Fitch's school opposite on Griswold Street (where as a young man Bishop Bissell had taught) attended one of our examinations – and, in return, a number of us girls went to the exercises which closed their term. I remember vividly the incisive clean-cut enunciation of Anson Burlingame in delivering a Latin oration.[64]

---

62. According to one male author's reminiscence, EH was among the "fair daughters" known as "Fort Street Girls" who "presented as brilliant a galaxy of feminine youth and beauty as could be found west of Albany." Friend Palmer, *Early Days in Detroit* (Detroit: Hunt & June, 1906), 934-935.

63. *Recollections*, 67-69. Maria Forsyth (1801-1882) married Benjamin B. Kercheval (1793-1855) in 1821, in Detroit. Frederick Marryat (1792-1848) included his perceptions of Michigan in the 1839 publication *A Diary in America, with Remarks on Its Institutions* (Paris: A. & W. Galignani & Co.). Samuel A. McCoskry (1804-1886) was first Episcopal Bishop of Michigan. The first Capitol of Michigan (both as Territory and State) was in a triangle park at Griswold and State Streets. Construction of Fort Wayne on the Detroit River began in 1842.

64. William Henry Augustus Bissell (1814-1893), Episcopal bishop. Anson Burlingame (1820-1870) was a student at the University of Michigan, 1838-

Much attention was paid to reading, writing and spelling. To misspell a word in writing a letter or note was considered a disgrace. It was a great delight to me to take up the study of Geometry in my Detroit school but I remember it was an open question with some of our friends whether the studies of a school-girl should include Geometry and Chemistry which I had also begun. I studied the first four books of Euclid, covering plane Geometry.[65]

My Father died 17th February, 1838. He had then been one and a half years out of active army life but his death was the direct result of his exposure and ill-treatment as a prisoner and of his resulting illness in Boston. His knee was bent and stiff. He tripped at the head of a flight of icy stairs leading down from Judge Hand's office on Jefferson Avenue. He was carrying at the time a large registry book for some verification and, being unable to recover himself, from his lameness, he was thrown to the foot. ... After my Father's death my Mother made our home with Uncle Forsythe.

I remember well my Father's reading every Sunday afternoon out of a big commentary which he held on his knees. It has always seemed to me as though he were searching after the truth but with no one to guide him.

It was a characteristic of my Father whenever he said anything quizzical or amusing to look down demurely, pursing his lips and stroking his chin softly. After his death I most often recalled him in this attitude. I have no recollection of ever receiving from my Father one harsh answer or one rough word.[66] ...

In the Autumn of 1838 I went to school at Utica, N.Y., where I remained a year. The principal of this Utica school was a Miss Sheldon, a wise and judicious woman with a remarkable power to enforce discipline. I greatly admired her and worked hard to win her approbation.

1841; as a Member of Congress, he denounced the attack in 1856 by Congressman Preston Brooks of South Carolina on Massachusetts Senator Charles Sumner in well-publicized remarks that led to a challenge for a duel.
65. Abraham Lincoln (and Robert E. Lee) studied Euclid.
66. *Recollections*, 69-71. George E. Hand (1809-1889) was probate judge.

In this I think I succeeded, for on my return home I received an invitation to come back to the school as teacher. This I would have done had it not been for the coming into my life of Dr. Tripler. ... My Father's death opened my spiritual eyes and softened my heart. ... I was baptised in old St. Paul's, Detroit (Woodward Avenue), by Bishop McCoskry and confirmed by him shortly after my marriage and just before my first child's birth. I thought with horror of giving birth to a child as an unbaptised woman. I said to the Bishop, "I don't know that I am prepared." "Oh, ask your husband. He is a good man."[67] ...

Gen. Scott, then commanding our Army, was accustomed each year to go over his old battle-fields and used to invite people right and left to accompany him. In the Summer of 1840, at Buffalo, he picked up an Adjutant and a regimental band of fifteen pieces and with these and his own suite came to Detroit. He called on Mrs. Clitz, whose husband, Capt. Clitz, had been his personal friend. At the time I happened to be visiting Miss Clitz (afterward Mrs. Pratt) for a week.[68] Of course Gen. Scott came in with great bluster. "Oh, this is one of my girls. Oh, both these are my girls. You must both join our party up the lakes." At the time I had a sty on my eye and would have preferred to remain at home. But Miss Clitz added her entreaties: "Oh, yes, we must go. It won't cost us anything." And we went – by the large steamer "Illinois" – to Mackinac and then to the Sault.[69] Gen. Scott drank champagne and at every meal informed us it was "the only wine my doctor allows me." My Uncle Kercheval was a passenger on the steamer from Mackinac to the Sault. He came to me and said, "Do you know your fare has not been paid? This I learned from the clerk." My Uncle, accordingly, paid my fare and certain

---

67. *Recollections*, 72-73. The Utica Female Academy opened in 1837. St. Paul's was on Woodward Avenue between Congress and Larned; in 1851, the church removed to a new structure at the corner of Congress and Shelby. Since 1907, its location has been 4800 Woodward Avenue.
68. John Clitz, Captain, 2nd U.S. Infantry, veteran of War of 1812, died at Fort Mackinac in 1836. "Miss Clitz" here refers to Mary; her future husband was also in the U.S. military.
69. Mackinac Island; Sault Ste. Marie, Michigan.

officers clubbed together and paid Miss Clitz' fare. At Mackinac, the Commandant, Dr. Harvey Brown[70], had a pretty daughter and Gen. Scott insisted that she, too, should be taken in the party to the Sault. But no arrangement was made for the paying of her fare until, again, a circle of officers provided for it. Naturally, all who knew these facts were indignant at Gen. Scott for his meanness. As for myself, I cut quite loose from him when I understood I was not his guest. At each meal he would say, "Miss Hunt, everyone is bound to eat fish when fish like these are to be had." "Thank you," I would reply, "I prefer whortle-berries."[71] And I did. I was very mad. We young people did have a merry time, however. Our steamer could, of course, go no farther North than the Sault – but we all went fifteen miles by schooner out into Lake Superior.[72] We had a dance on the shore and got ravenously hungry. Joe Johnston, a lieutenant[73], had joined us at the Sault. He said, "Why here's wood. Let's toast some bacon." And this we did, eating it with soda crackers. Lieut. Johnston toasted mine, kneeling on the sand. His manners were delightful. He was constantly thoughtful of others. On my return I wrote some doggerel about the trip which greatly amused my Cousin, Henry I. Hunt.[74] One stanza recounted many of our sights on land and water and ended:

"I have looked on a scene still greater, I wot,

---

70. Captain, Company H, 4th U.S. Artillery, which reoccupied Fort Mackinac on May 18, 1840. Edwin O. Wood, *Historic Mackinac: The Historical, Picturesque and Legendary Features of the Mackinac Country* (New York: Macmillan Co., 1918), 473, 481.
71. A wild berry ranking with blueberries in popularity during this era.
72. The first locks at Sault Ste. Marie opened in 1855.
73. In 1840, Joseph E. Johnston was 1st Lieutenant in the Topographical Engineers, on duty to survey the border with Canada and recommend locations for military fortifications. Craig L. Symonds, *Joseph E. Johnston: A Civil War Biography* (New York: W.W. Norton & Co., 1994), 47-48.
74. Henry Jackson Hunt. The text invariably substitutes "I" for "J", ostensibly because of the older H.J. Hunt having written that initial in a "peculiar manner." Palmer, 405.

For I've met that old humbug, Gen. Scott."[75]

IV. Early Married Life

In this portion, an unlikely romance begins to unfold between a 34-year old Army doctor from New York and an 18-year old who had come to Detroit only four years previous. It is the shortest chapter and ends with less-than-personal stories.

Dr. Tripler was ordered to Detroit from Buffalo in January, 1840, and drove over—a week or more en route—with a servant. He had a beautifully varnished black sleigh with red cushions and a fine team,—all greatly admired by the people of Detroit. He brought a small trunk, a gun case and a flute—but not many books as I remember. A piano came by boat in the Spring. After our first introduction I saw him every day in spite of his duties all over the city in attending officers. Uncle Forsythe had known him in Florida and wanted the match. Dr. Tripler would manifest the greatest interest in Uncle's horses or poultry and then would come into the house for a toddy or to ask after the ladies. Sometimes in the spirit of mischief I would not go to receive him, but get my Mother to appear in my place. This would bring a note from him on return to the city, so that he either saw me or had word directly from me each day. On the announcement of our engagement, the commanding officer in Detroit, Major Morris, gave us a dinner. Senator Norvell[76] proposed my health, which was drunk by all present. As I touched my lips to the glass I choked violently. My confusion was from my constant fear of appearing too young for Dr. Tripler. Mrs. Morris oversaw the preparation of Dr. Tripler's trousseau – for gentlemen's furnishings were not readily obtainable and had to

---

75. *Recollections*, 73-75.
76. John Norvell (1789-1850), U.S. Senator 1837-1841.

be made in each case specially. Dr. Tripler had treated and cured a child of Major and Mrs. Morris and their gratitude was very keen.

I was married in old St. Paul's Church on Woodward Avenue by Bishop McCoskry, 2 March, 1841 – two days before the inauguration of Harrison and Tyler.[77] Dr. Farnsworth was married just before us.[78] It was an evening wedding, followed by a reception and supper at Uncle Forsythe's. We had four bridesmaids and four groomsmen, all officers of the army. These were: Lieut. Clarke, Dr. Southgate, Lieut. Solle, Lieut. Tom Williams, the father of Bishop G. Mott Williams, and my Sister Ellen, Miss Eliza Woodbridge, Miss Martha Jones and Miss Belle Norvell, daughter of Senator Norvell. Dr. Southgate and Miss Woodbridge meeting first at our wedding, were afterward married.

For a few months after our marriage we boarded on Fort St. and then kept house in what all Detroiters called "The Parsonage" on Woodbridge St. back of Christ Church. ... Our family consisted of Dr. Tripler and myself and our three negro servants.[79] ...

I decided to keep a household expense-book and my husband rolled in a fit of uncontrollable laughter when he saw I had entered on one line, "Loaned to myself" and "Paid to myself."

Gen. Scott came to see us after our first child was born.[80] I must admit I was quite awed by his rank. He said to me concerning the baby, "And has your husband a theory? Because if he has, this child is ruined." Gen. Scott and Dr. Tripler used to play chess. If the General saw the game going against himself he would joggle the table and upset the board.

In offering his arm to a lady, Gen. Scott would always say, "Excuse this one, but my wound at Lundy's Lane compels me." It disgusted all

---

77. William Henry Harrison (1773-1841), 9th President of the United States, succeeded in office by John Tyler (1790-1862) upon his death after thirty-one days in office.
78. James Harvey Farnsworth (1818-1895) married Catherine Elizabeth Connor (1821-1902).
79. *Recollections*, 77-79.
80. Charles Stuart Tripler was born on May 8, 1842 in Detroit.

who knew that the real hero of Lundy's Lane was Gen. Brady[81], who never referred to the battle—nor had he need to. Old Gen. Brady was one of our intimate friends. One day he paid me a "compliment," as he called it: "Yes, you are a smart woman: you can do three things at once; you can knit and scold and rock the cradle." We lived in our first house a year and then went to Congress St., two doors west of Shelby. There my eldest child died and there Allie was born.[82] These two were but nineteen months apart. We moved next to Jefferson Avenue, opposite the Biddle House[83]. We were there but two months when Dr. Tripler left for the Mexican War. I stayed the year out and then lived with my Sister, now Mrs. Bissell, on the River Road at about 13th St.[84] ... Thence we went to the house we first occupied after our marriage at the corner of Cass and Fort, now kept by a Mrs. Moore, and boarded there till Dr. Tripler returned from Mexico.[85] ... The winter of 1838 to '39 was uncommonly severe in Michigan. The cold was intense and long-continued and the snow lay deep on the ground.[86] ...

In my childhood in Detroit, I remember well that on Election Day, each year, women and children had to keep closely within doors. This was from the general drunkenness that prevailed and the brawls

---

81. Hugh Brady (1768-1851), for whom the Brady Guards, a Detroit militia group, was named. Battle of Lundy's Lane, July 25, 1814, near Niagara Falls, Ontario.
82. The infant died on September 7, 1843, just three months before Alice Hunt Tripler's birth on December 19, 1843, in Detroit. She was named for her grandmother and nicknamed "Allie."
83. A prestigious Detroit hotel on Randolph Street between Jefferson and Woodbridge. The Millender Center now occupies the site. Their house was at Jefferson and Brush, just to the east. James H. Wellings, *Directory of the City of Detroit; and Register of Michigan, for the Year 1846* (Detroit: A.S. Williams, 1846), 141 (the publisher was Alpheus Starkey Williams of Civil War fame, who was then a newspaper publisher).
84. The River Road was alternatively known as Jefferson Avenue. This site, west of downtown, is just beyond the terminus of the Detroit River Walk. The Bissell and Tripler families were related by marriage.
85. The 1891 Detroit Club structure remains at that intersection.
86. *Recollections*, 79-81.

and street fights that always marked the day. In the old army, after the business of each day, many of the older officers were accustomed to give themselves to drink—and it was a dreadful example to those younger, who didn't like to be called "milk-sops." It would be said of a man, "He is not a drinking man. He is never drunk before dinner." It seemed that all that could be expected of a man was that he should keep sober in the morning. Common descriptive terms were "a one-bottle man," "a two-bottle man."[87]

V. Dr. Charles Stuart Tripler
This section begins with EHT's biographical sketch of CST's parents and his early life. We do not learn why he "long had an ambition to be an Army surgeon." He would spend his entire career – 36 years – in the uniform of his country. Most were as a happily married man.

Dr. Tripler's father had been a successful merchant in New York. As he prospered, he invested in land, then comparatively cheap. He sold his estate on Orchard St. and went farther North. At last Dr. Tripler's two half-brothers became involved in business entanglements and got their Father to become their security. They failed and he lost his whole fortune, the creditors taking even the family silver with the crest. This I learned from Madame Tripler, for Dr. Tripler never referred to the matter from mortification at his Father's and Brothers' conduct. These Brothers went to South America. The reverse in family affairs was so sudden and complete it caused a revulsion in all plans, and my husband, then only a little boy, but in active preparation for college, was apprenticed to an apothecary, a Mr. Stephen Brown. This man was a true friend and took a lively interest in his little clerk and oversaw his evening studies in his room, for he did study after working hours. He was a good Latin scholar and used to boast he never learned the meaning of one Latin word after he was twelve. It had all been flogged

---

87. *Recollections*, 81-82.

into him before, he said, by his teacher, a man named Barry. Mr. Stephen Brown had the degree of M.D. and, on my husband's graduation, he proposed they should form a partnership. I do not know just the terms he proposed, but my husband had other ambitions and declined the offer.

Dr. Tripler, when a little boy in New York, heard songs in the street calling on the citizens to defend themselves against the British. This was during the War of 1812.[88] ...

Dr. Tripler's father in New York was once made to sleep with a small-pox patient—in the hope and expectation he would have the disease in a mild form, but he did not have it at all. While a resident physician at Bellevue Hospital Dr. Tripler took the varioloid[89] and, through life, his face showed the marks. He was very ill. His mother, going out to see him at the hospital, overheard a passenger in the stage say, "Well, young Tripler died last night." This, however, proved hardly to be the case.[90] ...

Dr. Tripler's entrance into the Army was on this wise. He had long had an ambition to be an Army surgeon. The year of his graduation as M.D. from Columbia College, New York, he was written to by a Dr. Walter V. Wheaton, an elderly surgeon of the Army then stationed at West Point and urged to come up to the Point to assist him somewhat in his duties and also to attend to what private practice there might be for him.[91] Up to this time medical appointments in the Army had been entirely by political favour and without examination. Dr. Tripler was the first candidate ever examined for the medical service. The Secretary of War, Eaton[92], came this year to West Point with his wife. At a certain assembly this Dr. Wheaton introduced young Dr. Tripler to Mrs. Eaton and he danced with her. In some way she learned his

88. *Recollections*, 83-84.
89. I.e., he contracted smallpox.
90. *Recollections*, 85-86.
91. CST graduated from the College of Physicians and Surgeons, affiliated with Columbia University in lower Manhattan, in 1827. Wheaton (1786-1860) served as an instructor on the faculty of the U.S. Military Academy.
92. John H. Eaton (1790-1856).

ambition to enter the Army and his great desire for an appointment to be examined. On her return to Washington this appointment was immediately sent to Dr. Tripler[93]—and by her influence as was well known. Mrs. Eaton had a very humble origin. She had been a Miss Timberlake of Tennessee.[94]

While Dr. Tripler was at West Point he took the full mathematical course of the cadets. He, also, in these years, perfected himself in French. This West Point discipline had doubtless a lasting influence on Dr. Tripler as an officer. While at West Point, some of the companions of Dr. Tripler entered on an almost riotous bout. They took a cadet who had become entirely intoxicated, dead drunk in fact, and put him in a coffin, and, preceded by fife and drum, marched round the parade-ground. A Col. Vose was Commandant at the time and he inflicted for this proceeding no discipline at all—from his favouritism, as was said, for Dr. Tripler who was known to be in the company.[95] …

Dr. Tripler entered the Army at twenty-three, and, following West Point was stationed at Houlton and East-port, Maine. Then the Red River country and Baton Rouge.[96] Then Florida for the three Seminole campaigns.[97] There was much profane swearing in the Army and Gen. Harney[98], in particular, seemed to spend his time in making new and strange oaths. But in the Florida campaign, Dr. Tripler once riding alone in the deep forest was so struck with awe that he vowed never again to utter an oath. This vow he faithfully kept.[99] …

From Florida Dr. Tripler was ordered to Buffalo, and thence to Detroit. When my first child (a son) was born, Col. Childs who had served with Dr. Tripler at Tallahassee was God-Father and came on

---

93. His commission dated from October 30, 1830, when he was 23.
94. Margaret O'Neill (or O'Neale) Timberlake (1799-1879), Eaton's second wife.
95. *Recollections*, 87-89.
96. In Louisiana.
97. The so-called Second Seminole War, 1835–1842.
98. William S. Harney (1800-1889).
99. *Recollections*, 89.

from New York to Detroit for the Baptism. This son was Charles Stuart. He died at sixteen months.[100] …

VI. During the Mexican War

EHT recounts much about CST's experience during their first extended separation, the first of three intervals when his service necessitated her sacrifice. He would become acquainted with a number of officers whose names became familiar during the 1860s.

In 1846 Allie was two years old. She had had Cholera Infantum and Dr. Tripler said she must go to Mackinac. It was the month of June. When the news of the annexing of Texas was received, Dr. Tripler at once said "This means war with Mexico and a long separation for you and me." People who stay at home and make laws for other people to go out and fight, know nothing of the stern realities of the case.

Orders were received for the troops in Detroit to proceed to Mexico. Col. Reilley, in command, said, "We shall leave day after tomorrow." And they did—but very foolishly, for at Newport Barracks, Ken., they had to await for two weeks the troops coming from Eagle Harbour and Copper Harbour, Michigan. This Col. Reilley said, with what I thought was foolish bombast, "I'll earn a yellow sash or" (in form quoting Stark at Bennington) "Arabella Reilley is a widow."[101] Before starting, Dr. Tripler took my Mother and Allie to the Mackinac boat. To part from the child was like drawing his heart's blood. But it was inevitable. The regiment proceeded down the Ohio and Mississippi rivers and sailed from New Orleans. They had great discomfort and great danger as well, from unseaworthy transports. The landing was at Vera Cruz. An officer rushed to Gen. Scott: "General, they are firing on us." "Well, Sir, did I stipulate there should be no firing, Sir?"

A Capt. Albertis was killed there by a chance shell from the

---

100. *Recollections*, 90. Likely, Thomas Childs (1796–1853), West Point Class of 1814.
101. Bennett C. Riley (1787-1853), Colonel, 2nd U.S. Infantry.

"Castle." Mrs. Albertis was at Copper Harbour, Michigan, and did not learn of her husband's death for six months. Then she said "Well, half mourning will do for me. I didn't know my husband was dead for a whole half year."

The Army fought its way to the City of Mexico via Cerro Gordo, Molino del Rey, Chapultepec. Gen. Taylor[102] was advancing from the North to join forces. While on the way to Mexico City the Army was quartered in a certain town where Dr. Tripler made a very pleasant friendship with a physician of the place—and also with an aged Roman Priest. The latter he treated professionally. The old man, at their parting, wanted to pay Dr. Tripler for his services—but my husband said to him, "No. In my country the Clergy are treated free." The Priest replied "It is different here. In Mexico we pay double."

At last Gen. Scott entered Mexico City. Then I did not hear from my husband for six months for the Mexicans were in the rear of the American Army and all communication was cut. I got a scrawl from Cerro Gordo. Later a number of officers, including Dr. Tripler, hired a Mexican, at a great price, to carry a little packet of papers, in his boot-heel, to the coast. Each officer could send but a few lines. But none of these letters came through. The Army remained in the City of Mexico eight months. Dr. Tripler studied Spanish and learned it so that he enjoyed "Don Quixote" in the original. There was a Doctor Martinez whose acquaintance he valued and a little coterie of German merchants. With them Dr. Tripler saw his first Christmas Tree. When he came home he wanted me to have one. I said "No. Give me some woolen stockings and I will stuff them." I hated novelties.

One day while Dr. Tripler was pegging away at his Spanish Grammar he heard loud talking in the yard, and, looking out, saw his boy "Jim" from New York engaged in a violent quarrel with a Mexican boy—of course all in Spanish. While Dr. Tripler had been learning the Spanish grammar, Jim had been learning the Spanish language.[103]

---

102. Zachary Taylor (1784-1850), 12th U.S. President.
103. Unfortunately, Jim's identity is unknown.

Field hospitals in the Mexican War always showed the yellow flag—but this was made the special mark of the Mexican gunners. On one occasion, on a battlefield, Dr. Tripler was in the act of amputation and kneeling on the ground, when his patient, almost in his arms, as it were, was instantly killed—struck by a large fragment of rock which was hurled from a cliff by the bursting of a shell.

After the capture of Mexico a service of Thanksgiving was held. The Rev. Dr. McCarthy, a Churchman and Chaplain, celebrated the Holy Communion. A little band of officers communicated, at their head Gen. Scott. Major Duncan Stewart, a Paymaster, once told me Dr. Tripler saved more souls than any other man in Mexico—by doing, rather than saying, the right thing. "His life," he said "was a perpetual sermon." He added "Your husband brought me to the Church and to the Communion." This Major Stewart made his First Communion in New York City and, on that occasion, at his earnest request, Dr. Tripler knelt on one side of him and Gen. Robert Anderson (of Fort Sumter fame)[104] on the other. Dr. Tripler discouraged gambling among the officers and always threw his influence on the safe side. He did not object to card-playing.

On the march to Mexico City the sick and wounded were put by Dr. Tripler's order in the Churches which, fortunately, were without permanent seats and which were the only available places of shelter. In this disposition Dr. Tripler was as careful and reverent as it was possible to be. He always encouraged the Priests to screen the Altars and protect their furnishings—but, even so, there was much desecration.

Dr. Tripler was attached as Medical Director to the staff of Gen. Twiggs who commanded the Second Brigade of regular troops. At Pueblo he made an exhaustive report on the cause of the diseases prevailing in the Army. On the surrender and occupation of Mexico City, the duty of organizing and taking charge of the general hospital was assigned to Dr. Tripler. The buildings occupied for this purpose were

---

104. Colonel Robert Anderson (1805-1871), West Point Class of 1825, commanded the Federal garrison in Charleston Harbor in 1860-1861, and was subsequently promoted.

the Bishop's Palace, the Governor's Palace, the Iturbide Palace, the Inquisition, the College of Mines and the Convent of Santa Isabella. There was great lack of medical officers, most of the volunteer surgeons proving inefficient—and the distance from the United States preventing easy re-supply. It was what Dr. Tripler observed in the conduct of this campaign in Mexico as to the needs of the Medical Corps and the Army generally that induced him to prepare the Manuals he afterwards printed.[105] ...

While the "Army of Occupation" was in the City of Mexico religious services were regularly held by Father McCarthy, Priest of the Church and Chaplain. Among those perfectly regular in attendance were Gen. Scott, R.E. Lee[106], F.J. Porter[107], E.D. Townsend[108], Gen. Casey[109], Col. Gardiner[110] and Dr. Tripler. At the monthly Communion Gen. Scott, Dr. Tripler and some others always received. My husband used always to uncover his head if in the presence of the Host carried by Roman Catholic Priests through the streets. Some of his brother officers used to deride him for this, but, of course, he was not affected by their attitude.[111] ...

The "Aztec Club"[112] was organized in Mexico City to furnish a place of comfortable resort for the officers in the evening. Gen. Buchanan wanted billiards introduced. This was granted. Then he

---

105. *Recollections*, 93-97.
106. Robert E. Lee (1807-1870), West Point Class of 1829, most prominent Confederate General in the Civil War.
107. Fitz John Porter (1822-1901), West Point Class of 1845, Major-General in the Army of the Potomac.
108. Edward D. Townsend (1817-1893), West Point Class of 1837, Chief-of-Staff to General Scott and Assistant Adjutant-General, 1861-1863. The Triplers named a child after Townsend.
109. Silas Casey (1807-1882), West Point Class of 1826, Brigadier-General in the Army of the Potomac, 1861-1862.
110. John W.T. Gardiner (1817-1879), West Point Class of 1840, 1st Lieutenant in the 1st Dragoons during the Mexican-American War.
111. *Recollections*, 98-99.
112. The Aztec Club of 1847 was modeled after the Society of the Cincinnati, the Revolutionary War fraternity, as an association of commissioned officers who served during this war.

and his friends proposed gaming and drinking. Gen. Scott sent for Dr. Tripler and said "These men will get together enough votes to carry their schemes against us." Dr. Tripler snapped his teeth together and replied "I'll see to that" and he did. For night after night Dr. Tripler and his friends would attend the Club (giving up all other social engagements) and by their constant presence they prevented the proposed action. All this Major Stewart told me in New York City in 1864 one evening while calling on us—Dr. Tripler being on duty and away from our hotel.[113] …

On one occasion Fitz John Porter (then Captain) and Dr. Tripler passed, without knowing it, beyond the lines and found themselves within a very short distance of the Mexican camp. "And" Dr. Tripler said "We made rapid time back. Porter had the longer legs but I think I beat him." Dr. Tripler realized the Mexican War was a contest in which the heart of the American people was but little enlisted, chiefly because it was felt the war had resulted from the demand of the slave-holding South for more territory. However, he used to say the time would come when the nation would more truly appreciate the brilliancy of the campaign under Scott, a campaign without a defeat and almost, as one might say, without a check.[114] …

Once at a Court Martial at Jefferson Barracks, Mo., Dr. Tripler gave testimony as to the general good character of a certain soldier and he closed by saying, characteristically, "I think when a man fights as well as I've seen this man fight in Mexico, he's got a perfect right to get drunk, if he wants to."

Dr. Tripler read the Medical works of Spanish, French and Italian authors. He once said it was especially interesting to note the scientific progress of the Italians. This rather surprised me.

While my husband was in Mexico I was one afternoon shocked by two men climbing a high board fence at the side of our house (Jefferson Avenue) and peering into the room where I was dressing.

---

113. *Recollections*, 99-100.
114. *Recollections*, 100-101.

I instantly drew the shade. There was a pistol in the house and the next afternoon I laid it in full view on a table directly in front of the window. After dressing I raised the shade. As I anticipated, the men at once appeared again on the fence. I simply bowed my head and pointed dramatically to the pistol. They dropped as though shot and it ended the annoyance.

This house had a front porch only three or four steps above the Avenue. One evening a drunken man came tumbling up upon the porch and into the front door which closed behind him. Seeing his condition, I said "You must get right out of here." He hiccoughed "But you see I've come to stay." I passed rapidly round him and opened the door. Then quickly facing him I threw myself against him with all my young strength. He fell down those steps into the street, seemingly end over end. It is surprising to note the result of sudden power when applied unexpectedly.

I remember meeting Zachary Taylor in Detroit in the early forties, when he was visiting his cousin, James Taylor, a Colonel in the Army who lived at the time on Jefferson Avenue. This Col. Taylor had married a daughter of Judge McLean of the U. S. Supreme Court. Judge McLean I also met. He was a remarkably sober man, seeming to carry a weighty responsibility into the very minutiae of life. You could never joke with him. Zachary Taylor himself was very rough in his demeanor and not at all like a gentle man in his mode of address.[115]

The Grants came to Detroit in 1849.[116] Mrs. Grant and I exchanged calls. U.S. Grant was then a Lieutenant in the Army and

---

115. *Recollections*, 101-103.
116. Ulysses S. Grant (1822-1885), West Point Class of 1843, future General in command of the Armies of the United States, 18th U.S. President; Julia Dent Grant (1826-1902); they married August 22, 1848. They lived in a house at 253 East Fort Street between Rivard and Russell streets. The structure is owned by the State of Michigan and in the process of relocation and restoration. Another notable event of 1849 for the community was the formation of the Wayne County Medical Society, which still exists. EHT's husband helped found the organization and was its first vice-president. Paul Leake, *History of Detroit*, Vol. I (Chicago: Lewis Pub. Co., 1912), 417.

his pay was about $60 per month. Dr. Tripler was at this time a Major. Mrs. Grant always had a great lump of a baby in her arms.[117] Dr. Tripler pointed out Grant to me in the street one day. "That's Grant over there. How he does drive that little rat of a horse" (a French pony, a pacer—though the best he could afford. At this very time, as I well remember, Dr. Tripler was driving his pair of Vermont Morgan mares). Grant used to drive furiously on Jefferson Avenue then unpaved and on the River Rouge when frozen. And we met the Grants in company occasionally. I recall, in particular, a large party at Gen. Brady's where they were present. Most of the time Lieut. Grant was standing rather aloof from the company and uncommunicative with his hands behind his back, impassive. He always gave me the impression of a school-boy who had not learned his lesson, but he was always very devoted and tender to his wife. She, as I think, was his salvation. My cousin, Capt. Lewis Hunt[118], a class-mate of Grant at West Point, had said to me, "There's more in Grant than you think."[119]

I had no personal acquaintance with S.B. Buckner[120] but I know that his was a very lovable character. I knew the daughter of Major Kingsbury whom he married and a beautiful young woman she was.

I knew Lieut. J.C. Pemberton[121] as an Artillery Officer in Detroit.

---

117. The Grants' first child, Frederick Dent Grant, was born May 30, 1850, in St. Louis. Army Surgeon Tripler provided Julia Grant with medical counsel during her pregnancy in Detroit. John Y. Simon ed., *The Personal Memoirs of Julia Dent Grant* (New York: G.P. Putnam's Sons, 1975), 66. The Triplers' fourth child, Ellen Mackintosh, was born in Detroit on September 8, 1849. She died on October 8, 1850.
118. Lewis Cass Hunt (1824-1886), West Point Class of 1847, Colonel of the 92nd New York Infantry, participated in the Peninsula Campaign in 1862, being wounded in the Battle of Seven Pines on May 31-June 1, 1862.
119. *Recollections*, 103-104.
120. Simon B. Buckner (1823-1914), West Point Class of 1844, surrendered the Rebel garrison at Fort Donelson, Tennessee, to Grant on February 16, 1862.
121. John C. Pemberton (1814-1881), West Point Class of 1837, surrendered the Confederate forces defending Vicksburg, Mississippi, to Grant on July 4, 1863.

This was a little before the Grants came in 1849. Lieut. Pemberton was of haughty demeanor and by no means popular.

I knew Joe Johnston when he was a Captain of the Topographical Engineers. After we removed to Detroit he came to Michigan also and in company with Capt. Canfield[122] and three civilians, went to the Upper Peninsula on topographical work. He had a most engaging manner and charmed everybody. I think he was, at this time, in love with Mary Canfield and he used to come to our home in Detroit in the hope to find her there.[123]

VII. *The California Service*
EHT would endure four years apart from her husband during his service on the West Coast. Her husband would come to know U.S. Grant better, and he would share his insights when they reunited.

In 1850 the Army post at Detroit was broken up.[124] We went at once to Fort Gratiot[125] which was delightful in summer. There were but two companies at that post. Communication with Detroit was by boat or team. I went from Fort Gratiot down to Detroit to see the city in its first illumination by gas street-lamps. This was thought to be very

---

122. Augustus Canfield (1800-1854), West Point Class of 1822, married Mary Sophia Cass (1812-1882), a daughter of Lewis Cass.
123. *Recollections*, 104.
124. The 1850 Census records the "Trippler" family in Detroit, Charles in the profession of "U.S. Surgeon" with his wife "Uniz" and three children: 6-year old Alice H., 4-year old Charles, and 3-year old Ellen M. (along with three unrelated Irish natives). Ellen Mackintosh, their fourth, was born in Detroit on September 8, 1849, and died on October 8, 1850, not long after the census taker's visit. This boy was given his name after Charles, the couple's first child, had died, a not uncommon practice of that era.
125. A Federal military installation in Saint Clair County, Michigan, along the St. Clair River. The Triplers' fifth child, Ellen Cass, was born there on August 21, 1851; she died on February 11, 1930. A survey of its history (mentioning Dr. Tripler) was published in the *Detroit Free Press* on August 24, 1890, page 13. The Post Hospital is the only surviving structure, located in Lighthouse Park in Port Huron.

wonderful as an improvement. When we first came to Detroit in 1836 there were scarcely any street lamps—even of oil—except a few just before the principal hotels.

Once Dr. Tripler drove my Mother in winter from Detroit to Fort Gratiot. The Commanding Officer at Fort Gratiot was Gabriel I. Raines.[126] He was an unpopular man and spent most of his time experimenting with electricity. Mrs. Raines was a Southern woman and was representative of household shiftlessness. One evening, I remember, we were invited to the Raines house and our entertainment consisted of egg-nog which was served to us from a tin watering-pot. I concluded that no pitcher being available, appeal had been taken to the gardener.

At the out-break of the Civil War, Raines promptly joined the Confederate Army. On the evacuation of Richmond in 1865 he arranged, on a table in some central or public hall, a pitcher and glasses, in such wise as to tempt the first officers entering to drink. He then joined the rebel force in flight. But the suspicions of the Federal Officers were aroused and an investigation followed. The table was found to be connected by wires with a magazine of powder. It was the deed of a fiend and universally execrated. It was contrary to the rules of warfare and Raines was a trained soldier. It was against civilization for the whole country, South as well as North, had for months foreseen that the capture of Richmond meant the end of strife. It was against the instincts of humanity for it was a stab at his former brother officers.

It was while at Fort Gratiot that orders came to Dr. Tripler to go to California. The troops went by Steamer from New York though Dr. Tripler thought it a great cruelty to start them at a season when cholera was raging on the Isthmus. It was June, 1852. The crossing of

---

126. Gabriel James Rains (1803-1881), West Point Class of 1827, became a Brigadier-General in the Confederate Army. He was in charge of the "Torpedo Bureau" and inventor of various explosive devices. John H. Eicher & David J. Eicher, *Civil War High Commands* (Stanford: Stanford University Press, 2001), 443-444.

the Isthmus was fearful. Shiploads of laborers for the railway died as fast as they came—or, as the saying was, "An Irishman for every tie." Miasma and pestilence were everywhere. The troops went by boat up the Chagres River which was covered with a heavy, green slime. Then they marched through mud so deep it was soberly said certain soldiers were actually lost in the mud and never found. Of course this meant that sometimes, while on the march, soldiers were attacked with cholera, and, being unable to keep their place in column, would lie down in the mud. Death at times came swiftly after the commands had passed on. Dr. Tripler said, when some such cases of sudden seizure were reported to him, he rode back to give relief but could find no patient at the point indicated. Out of 700 men, women and children, 70 died on the Isthmus and Dr. Tripler was their only surgeon. But a ship's surgeon at Aspinwall, for very pity's sake, crossed with Dr. Tripler to give him aid. The officer who so volunteered was Dr. Elisha Kent Kane, afterward of Arctic fame.[127] It was an [sic] heroic deed and appreciated by Dr. Tripler who had unbounded admiration for Kane. Years after, some time following Kane's return from the far North, the two met in Cincinnati and renewed their friendship.

Before leaving New York, Dr. Tripler wrote the Surgeon General it was murder to attempt the crossing of the Isthmus then. But the reply was it would be "quickly over." I wrote to my husband in New York to let me join him. Other officers' wives were going. He answered "Should you come I could not give you a moment of my time." The Panama Railway was not finished till two years later. In going to such a place a surgeon knows his own peril. I cannot believe Dr. Tripler ever dreamed a canal across the Isthmus would one day be attempted.[128]

In Panama Bay the sick were put aboard a certain vessel to which were also assigned, by order of the Commanding Officer, a Col. Bonnerville, all the women and children. This Col. Bonnerville was a very stupid man mentally—appointed from civil life. The only

---

127. Elisha Kent Kane (1820-1857), medical officer in the U.S. Navy.
128. *Recollections*, 105-108.

medical officer in attendance was Dr. Tripler and he was worn out by his exhausting duties. He was indignant at the inhumanity which could so needlessly imperil the lives of the women and children. The hospital stewards, enlisted men, were extremely negligent of their duties to the sick and Dr. Tripler called for an officer each day to remain twenty-four hours and compel these men to do their duty and look out for deserters. The officer assigned one day to be with him in this way was Lieut. U.S. Grant. Another officer, Lieut. Gore, so detailed to assist Dr. Tripler died of the cholera on this ship. The soldiers hated the duty and confinement of the hospital ship and, in very many cases, promptly and quietly dropped over the side and swam ashore. Col. Bonnerville was greatly exercised at the action of Dr. Tripler and threatened to have him court-martialed. But Dr. Tripler told him he wished he would make his threat good for that he wanted nothing better than such an opportunity to let the full conditions be known. My husband's previous army experience in Maine, Arkansas and Florida had given him a wider outlook than that of most officers.[129]

Three months after Dr. Tripler left me Mr. Bissell died and I went at once to house-keeping and took my Mother and the Bissell family.

In San Francisco expenses were so great Dr. Tripler engaged in private practice for his own maintenance and sent me all his pay which I needed for the family in Detroit. At this time there was a mail to and from California but once a fortnight. An addition of two dollars per day to their regular pay was made to all officers in California to live on. U.S. Grant had a coal yard in San Francisco. Wallen had a milk route.[130] Turkeys cost $25 each. While in San Francisco in 1853 Dr. Tripler made a partnership for private practice with a Dr. Hewitt

---

129. An account, including Tripler's September 14, 1852, report to the Army's Surgeon-General (mentioning Bonnerville), is in Albert Edwards, *Panama: The Canal, the Country, and the People* (New York: Macmillan Co., 1912), 400-407. Benjamin L.E. Bonneville (1796-1878), West Point Class of 1815, wounded veteran of the Mexican-American War and recipient of a brevet promotion for gallant and meritorious conduct, was Lieutenant-Colonel of the 4th U.S. Infantry.

130. Henry D. Wallen (1819-1886), West Point Class of 1840, was on duty in Detroit during 1848-1850.

Plates

View of Washington, D.C. from the south, 1834. Library of Congress

Detail from the Capitol Rotunda painting showing Eunice Hunt as a child. Courtesy of Charles David Cullen

Etching of Eunice Hunt as a young woman. Courtesy of Tripler Medical Center, Honolulu, Hawaii

View of Detroit from Canada, circa 1837. Library of Congress

Eunice and child, from "a daguerreotype, taken about 1855". *Reminiscences*, after p. 110

Fort Gratiot post hospital, Port Huron, Mich., 2022. Courtesy of Dave Dempsey

Newport Barracks in Kentucky, on the Ohio River. *Harper's Weekly*, Aug. 31, 1861

The "Seven Buildings" in Washington, D.C., on Pennsylvania Avenue. Library of Congress

Charles Stuart Tripler in U.S. Army uniform during the Civil War. Courtesy of Charles David Cullen

Eunice Hunt Tripler on July 14, 1893. Courtesy of Charles David Cullen

MANUAL

OF

THE MEDICAL OFFICER

OF THE

ARMY OF THE UNITED STATES,

PART I.

RECRUITING AND THE INSPECTION OF RECRUITS.

BY

CHARLES S. TRIPLER, M.D.,

Surgeon U. S. A..; Fellow of the College of Physicians and Surgeons
of the University of the State of New York.

CINCINNATI:
WRIGHTSON & CO., PRINTERS, 167 WALNUT ST.
1858.

Title page of "Tripler's Manual."

Grave of Eunice Hunt Tripler, Elmwood Cemetery, Detroit. Editor's collection

of New York City. This continued about a year, when, for domestic reasons, Dr. Hewitt had to return to New York. Being in a strait for money he borrowed of Dr. Tripler $550. No part of this sum was repaid to Dr. Tripler though he told me in 1866 that he believed Dr. Hewitt was perfectly honest and, if he could get ahead in money matters, he would pay the debt. Some time after Dr. Tripler's death, I wrote Dr. Hewitt an exact statement of my financial condition and the burdens I had to carry. I told him of my husband's faith in him and I enclosed his note to Dr. Tripler for the $550—now outlawed. He replied immediately that when he made his next half-yearly collections he would remit the amount. And this he did, sending the money in greenbacks by express.

In 1854 Dr. Tripler was ordered to Benicia though really needed in San Francisco in his profession for consultation especially. The rule of Jefferson Davis[131], now Secretary of War, was "two years at a post." So there was no leaving for Dr. Tripler till 1856.

While in San Francisco Dr. Tripler was one of the vestry of Grace Church to greet Bishop Kip on his arrival and ask him to become its Rector. The Bishop asked the financial condition. "Well, Bishop, the sheriff is at the doors." The Bishop became Rector. At Benicia Dr. Tripler became a Lay Reader. Gen. Townsend and he clubbed together, hired and furnished a room for service, both were licensed by the Bishop and alternated in taking the service. A Miss Atkins, a Presbyterian, kept a boarding-school in the place. In some way her teacher of mathematics failed her. Dr. Tripler said to her cheerfully, "Why, I will take those classes." This kept the school from a breakdown. Of course this was done quite gratuitously and Dr. Tripler taught in this way for about a year. Naturally, Miss Atkins and her pupils came somewhat to the lay service. At last Dr. Tripler wrote to Bishop Kip there was a class of fourteen ready for Confirmation, instructed by himself. The Bishop came and confirmed them. This was

---

131. Jefferson Finis Davis (1808-1889), West Point Class of 1828, only President of the Confederate States of America.

the beginning of Church life in Benicia. Miss Atkins finally became a Communicant and her school developed into a Church institution.

In California Dr. Tripler was associated with U.S. Grant, W.T. Sherman[132], Joseph Hooker[133], E.D. Townsend. Hooker, at this time, was a gambler and drunkard. Grant was in my husband's care and Dr. Tripler was entirely frank and open in dealing with his case.[134] He, at last, resigned from the Army and came East. From the difference in rank, first in Dr. Tripler's favour and later in Grant's, there was hardly intimacy between the two.

From the savings of his private practice in California Dr. Tripler lent $3,000 and lost it. His loss resulted from his placing this money in the hands of Gen. Charles P. Stone[135], who had gone into the banking business in San Francisco and whose chief clerk, a son of Col. Cleary of the Army, proved to be an embezzler and fled with the funds of many officers. This was the Gen. Stone who was confined in Fort Warren, Boston Harbour, during the Civil War and who afterward became Stone Pasha of Egypt. Dr. Tripler had $1,700 when he got to Detroit. He returned East by the Isthmus and I met him in New York. We went on to Washington for three days, where Dr. Tripler reported and presented his returns and accounts. Then we hastened to Detroit, for Dr. Tripler wanted to see the children so much.

Some time in the year 1852, while Dr. Tripler was in California, I met the author, James Fenimore Cooper[136], at a dinner party at Gen.

---

132. William T. Sherman (1818-1891), West Point Class of 1840, Union Major-General during the Civil War.
133. Joseph Hooker (1814-1879), West Point Class of 1837, Union Major-General during the Civil War.
134. EH refers here to Grant's purported susceptibility to alcohol. The issue is recently treated in Ron Chernow, *Grant* (New York: Penguin Press, 2017), 127-129, as is Grant's West Coast financial activity.
135. Charles P. Stone (1824-1887), West Point Class of 1845, associated with the Union disaster at the Battle of Ball's Bluff, October 21, 1861.
136. James Fenimore Cooper (1789-1851), author of the *Leatherstocking Tales* and other classics of American literature.

Cass'. When I understood Cooper was to be present I tried to excuse myself, but Mrs. Cass insisted on my going.[137] ...

During Dr. Tripler's absence in California we one Summer had much more than the usual cholera scare. All our neighbours and friends fled—most of them going to Mackinac—the Canfields, Gen. Cass' family and all. From our home on Fort Street I could not see one house that was occupied, and most of the houses in this condition were entered and robbed. But I could not leave. I could not break up my family and abandon our house to be plundered. I was very nervous at night—but bold as a lion by day. I told a gentleman friend that if I had a pistol I believed I would entirely recover from the cholera scare. He brought me a pistol and taught me to use it by practice at a target in our back yard 130 feet off. I got so that at that distance he said I would be sure to hit a man—and I had much comfort in the thought. Of course every one knew I was pistol-practising from the sound of the firing. I felt much more secure and could, at last, sleep. My friends used to laugh at my new cure for the cholera scare. It was fortunate that the outbreak of the disease was late in the season, for frost soon brought immunity. However, I counted fourteen funerals passing our house one afternoon.[138]

The California duty separated my husband and me forty-six months.

While he was in California the wife of Senator Gwin[139] came to Dr. Tripler and tried to induce him to attend her husband on the dueling field. Dr. Tripler declined and sent word to the Senator not to go out. The Senator did not go. In this Dr. Tripler, of course, gave up an enormous fee.

Dr. Tripler never opposed beer-drinking nor wine-drinking by the soldiers at an army post, and I am entirely sure the modern movement

---
137. *Recollections*, 108-112.
138. EHT may have been referring to the time her home was broken into, and these may be the same period of time.
139. William M. Gwin (1805-1885), physician and one of California's first U.S. Senators.

for abolishing the "canteen" would have found no friend in him. He was the truest kind of a temperance man both in precept and example. For myself, I feel deeply that the soldier has a right to his light drinks. And it is, in my opinion, better to provide them at the post itself than to force the soldier to go for them outside. When he goes, he thinks he must improve the occasion by "filling up" on poor whiskey. When he knows by walking across the parade-ground he can get his beer at any time, he loses half his desire for it.

Dr. Tripler was associated with Gen. John E. Wool in California. Gen. Wool was a man of most egregious vanity and very unpopular with his brother officers and in the Army generally—but was quite obtuse to the fact. He, one day, dilated to Dr. Tripler on the subject of his own possible illness and death and the consequent trouble and care which would result to the command in the necessary arrangements for the funeral of an officer of his rank. Dr. Tripler long afterward used to chuckle over the reply he made. For he said, "Don't give the subject another thought, General. The officers will be simply delighted to attend to the matter." Gen. Wool looked rather wild at this.[140]

VIII. Newport, Kentucky

From 1856 to 1861, the Triplers lived at a duty station on the border between freedom and bondage along the Ohio River. Their first four children had been born in Detroit, followed by one born at Fort Gratiot. She would birth three more children in Kentucky, the birthplace of a lawyer three years younger than CST whose parallel five years would bring him into national prominence and to the White House. EHT is exposed to "the first secession sentiment" expressed to her directly and reveals her own sentiments.

In July, 1856, at Newport, Ky., Stuart, then twelve years old[141], was taken ill from eating cherries and then going to swim in the river. The

---

140. *Recollections*, 112-115.
141. Referring to Charles Stuart Tripler, who was born in 1846. See Appendix.

mosquitoes and the stifling heat were almost intolerable. I literally gave up my whole time to his care—though I was going to be confined in November. I watched with him, slept with him and carried him in my arms whenever he was to be moved. I would even run with him in my arms up and downstairs. I read to him nearly all of Scott's and Cooper's novels to keep him quiet. Dr. Tripler was, of course, much engaged with his lectures in the Cincinnati Medical College and his outside duties generally. But I lived with and for my boy—as I lived afterward with Dr. Tripler in his illness—and with Allie in hers. It is no wonder that now my heart is in tatters.[142] One thing surely was in my favour in these long physical strains. I could always eat heartily and with thankfulness that I had the ability.

During his five years at Newport Dr. Tripler studied Astronomy and often assisted Prof. Mitchell in his observations at Mount Adams[143]. The two men became very intimate from the similarity of their tastes.[144] ...

In the Winter of 1860 to '61 at Newport, Dr. Tripler wrote his "Handbook for Military Surgeons."[145] If this could have been generally circulated through the Medical Corps it would have been a great boon to the Army and country. Dr. Tripler later wrote by circular to all Medical officers under him to make formal requisitions for things

---

142. Charles predeceased EHT, dying on January 13, 1906, in Tacoma, Washington, after having served in the Union Army. See Appendix. Dr. Tripler died in 1866. Allie died on February 15, 1871, in Detroit.
143. The Cincinnati Observatory known by some as "Birthplace of American Astronomy." Ormsby M. Mitchel (1810-1862) was a Cincinnati College professor involved in its construction, as well as a Union Civil War General. The structure still exists.
144. *Recollections*, 117-118.
145. There are two editions of the *Hand-Book*, with Tripler identified as "A.M., M.D., Surgeon U.S. Army" (Cincinnati: Robert Clarke & Co., 1861). The Preface indicates that Tripler's contributions were based on lectures he gave "for the last three years" at the Medical College of Ohio and that his contributions were truncated because he "was summoned to report himself to headquarters before his revision of his labors was completed." His co-author was George Curtis Blackman (1819–1871), professor of surgery at the College.

needed. Sometimes these officers hardly knew what a requisition was. The Army needed an efficient General Staff. In "Gen. McClellan's Own Story" this is made very clear by him.[146]

It was while we were in Newport that I prevailed on my Mother to go to Washington and apply for a pension—for I felt the justice of her claim, though my Father had died actually out of the service. On this errand my Mother went to Washington in the Winter of 1858-'59. ... My Mother did not know exactly to whom to apply for help. But she knew the City of Washington and had hosts of Army friends. Still their advice was conflicting and confusing. My Mother, however, decided to see Jefferson Davis, Senator from Mississippi, who had been Secretary of War in Pierce's Cabinet, 1853 to '57. She called at the hotel where the Davises were staying. It proved to be their breakfast-hour. Mrs. Davis came forward and received my Mother. In a short time Mr. Davis also appeared with a newspaper in hand. Mrs. Davis introduced my Mother and stated her errand in a few words. My Mother took breakfast (or rather coffee, for she had breakfasted) with the Davises. They had a private table. My Mother's mode of speech was very touching and effective. She told Mr. Davis she wished to relieve Dr. Tripler of the burden of her care. Mr. Davis' advice was, "Go and see Mr. Crittenden (Senator from Kentucky)[147] and tell him your case just as you have told it to me, but don't tell him I sent you." This my Mother did. She afterward saw Jeff Davis at the Capitol and he gave her more advice, handing her a written list of a number of Congressmen whom she should see, and assuring her he had himself

---

146. George B. McClellan, *McClellan's Own Story: The War for the Union, the Soldiers Who Fought It, the Civilians Who Directed It and His Relations to It and to Them* (New York: Charles L. Webster & Co., 1887). The General's modern biographer referred to EHT's husband as "reform-minded" and, accordingly, McClellan's choice to work his will against the military bureaucracy. Stephen W. Sears, *George B. McClellan: The Young Napoleon* (New York: Da Capo Press, 1999), 127.

147. John J. Crittenden (1787-1863), U.S. Senator from Kentucky from 1855-1861, and advocate for the so-called "Crittenden Compromise" that sought to avert civil war during December 1860-March 1861.

seen a number in her interest. She saw Senator Seward of New York[148] and he said to her, "You had better see Senator Clay of Alabama.[149] If you can get him to say nothing when your case comes up in committee it will be a great advantage." Clay was on the Pension Committee. He said, "Mrs. Hunt, I have made it a rule never to vote for private pension bills. But your case is a just one. Yet I cannot break my rule." My Mother bowed her head and said simply, "I am so sorry." Senator Clay added, "I will do this: When your case comes up in Committee, I will leave the room." On the advice of friends, my Mother went on a certain day to the reception-room of the Committee on Pensions and waited there. Presently the door opened and Mr. Clay came out. He bowed to her in silence. My Mother knew then that her bill was being considered, and, soon, that it was favorably reported. It was an interesting occasion in the Senate when the bill was finally passed. Senator Crittenden proposed to increase the amount from that first recommended. This was at once agreed to.[150] Mr. Crittenden then rose and bowed in a stately way to my Mother who was seated in the gallery. He was a gentleman of the old school and this small act was graceful and gracious. In six weeks from the time she left home my Mother was back with the pension paid from the date of application. Jefferson Davis said to my Mother, "Mrs. Hunt, come to Washington next year and get your back pension" (from date of my Father's death). But "next year" brought other matters to Jefferson Davis. The pension granted my Mother was $420 per year, i.e., one-half the pay proper of a Captain at that time (other allowances were for forage, quarters,

---

148. William H. Seward (1801-1872), U.S. Senator from New York, Secretary of State from March 1861-March 1869.
149. Clement Claiborne Clay (1816-1882), U.S. Senator from Alabama, and member of the Confederate Senate.
150. On March 31, 1860, Senator Zachariah Chandler (see n. 186) brought the bill up on the floor of the Senate, and Crittenden proposed to increase the amount from $20 to $35, which was at that time a captain's monthly half-pay rate. The amendment passed, as did the bill. *Congressional Globe*, 36th Congress, 1st Session, 1467. It was signed into law by the 15th President, James Buchanan (1791-1868), on April 11. Id. 1647.

servant, transportation, etc.). The weak points in my Mother's application were, first, the fact that my Father was not in actual service at the time of his death. Secondly, the records of the War Department were burned in 1814 when the British took Washington. No records exist now in the Adjutant General's office back of that date. In 1859, however, Gen. Jessup was Quarter Master General.[151] He had been a companion and fellow-prisoner of my Father and gave his testimony as to this fact and as to their capture and exchange. The very next year Gen. Jessup died. Gen. Gibson, Commissary General[152], also testified to my Father's coming to Washington while suffering and his being long under treatment there. The testimony of these two was most helpful.[153]

When my Mother's bill passed, Gen. Palmer (of the Engineers) sent a telegram to Dr. Tripler (in Newport). The telegram read, "My bill passed half an hour ago. Four twenty per year." I saw Dr. Tripler open the envelope. He threw his cap into the air and cried out, "Hurrah for Grammy."

To this time Dr. Tripler had been giving to my Mother $200 per year, to my Sister Ellen $300 and to his own mother $200.

Dr. Tripler took an intense dislike to Jefferson Davis while Secretary of War. His orders were injudicious and tyrannical, arbitrary and hard to be carried out. I have often wondered why he treated my Mother so courteously and really believe her beauty had much to do with it.

When Jefferson Davis was confined in Fortress Monroe in 1865

---

151. Thomas S. Jesup (1788-1860), Quartermaster-General from 1818-1860. The file contains a letter of endorsement by Jesup, stating that he was the Adjutant-General of that Army and personally observed Hunt's "gallant and energetic" conduct.
152. George Gibson (1775-1861), Commissary-General of Subsistence from 1818-1861.
153. The application was also supported by Dr. Zina Pitcher (see n.202), testifying that Hunt's malady dated at least from 1830 due to his capitivity, and that his lameness had caused a fall that resulted in death.

and 1866 my son Stuart[154] was a Lieutenant and stationed there. As officer of the day he repeatedly walked by Mr. Davis' side when he was out for exercise. Stuart told Mr. Davis he was Mrs. Hunt's Grandson—whom Mr. Davis said he well remembered. My Mother wrote to Stuart to tell Jeff Davis she was still mindful of his kindness. This Stuart did, and Mr. Davis was much moved. Stuart said Mr. Davis was a very interesting man from the width of his information. One day he pointed out a little insignificant shrub growing on the ramparts. "That is so-and-so. It is good for such a purpose." He talked to Stuart one day about certain varieties of rare birds. On another occasion he gave him some prescriptions for certain horse diseases. They never talked of politics, but Stuart was impressed with the depth of Mr. Davis' sorrow and disappointment as a broken-spirited man.

At Newport in January, 1861, the wife of Col. James Ebert (formerly a Miss Taylor), being a rank secessionist, said to me, "Our Army is worthless; it has no spirit; it is the scum of the earth." I said to her, "Answer for yourself. My husband does not belong to the scum of the earth."

At this same time at the lowering of the flag at sundown, women secessionists of Newport would stamp and spit upon it, and an order was issued forbidding women to enter the grounds. A Col. James Taylor, cousin of President Zachary Taylor, announced that on a certain day he would have a flag-raising at his place, a few blocks distant, his house occupying a noble and commanding site. All his family were secessionists, and on this occasion Mrs. Taylor even drew down the curtains of the house and would not show herself. I attended this flag-raising—though really to accompany my daughter Allie, who teased to go and who was wearing the universal cockade of red, white and blue. Col. Taylor's speech was thrilling. He explained that he had selected this day as the anniversary of the day his Father's family had arrived in Newport after their long journey of hundreds of miles down the Ohio. He dwelt upon their constant danger from the Indians and

---

154. Charles Stuart Tripler, born in 1846. See Appendix.

the perils of their wilderness life while the journey lasted. "But on this day we saw a little flag which seemed hardly larger than a pocket-handkerchief, floating from this point against the blue sky—and then we knew we were safe—and we've been safe ever since. And shall we be ingrates now? Let the flag wave." And instantly the beautiful great standard went up. I was deeply moved.

Senator Crittenden followed. "You are going to let them drag Kentucky out of the Union. Then here will be the battle-field and you yourselves homeless. Do not be caught by these tricksters and designing men of the South."

The first secession sentiment I ever heard proclaimed was by a Major Macklin, a Paymaster, in Newport. I arose at once and said, "Well, this is the first disunion speech I have ever listened to:—and it is in my own house. I will excuse myself. Good evening, Major Macklin." And I withdrew.[155]

I never saw cruelty of any sort shown toward the slaves who were, as I remember them, universally cheerful and content. Dr. Tripler had a niece who, when a young married woman, visited us in Newport. She employed a poor colored woman, who had been a field hand in the South, as wet-nurse for her child. This negress was from the most ignorant and hopelessly degraded class. She was so strange to the interior of a house that she went upstairs on all fours, and in descending she would always back downward. I understood she had once been beaten with an iron poker for some act of insubordination—but I believe such treatment was very rare. Surely it should have been unknown.[156]

---

155. *Recollections*, 119-126. Sackfield Maclin (1809-1876) became part of the surrender of Federal property during the secession crisis in Texas in January 1861, including the arrest of the officer in charge of U.S. troops there, and would become a Confederate officer. Edward S. Cooper, *Traitors: The Secession Period, November 1860-July 1861* (Madison: Fairleigh Dickinson University Press, 2008), 77-90.

156. *Recollections*, 126. EHT's naiveté toward the real conditions of human bondage in the slave States contrasts with her categorical opposition to its cruelty.

Gen. William T. Sherman we used to see frequently while at Newport. He was often at our house. In California Dr. Tripler had attended his little son when ill, and, as Gen. and Mrs. Sherman always said, saved his life. The first time the Shermans came to our house in Newport Col. Sherman stood the little fellow on a chair, and, speaking in the first person as in the boy's stead, made a little speech of gratitude to Dr. Tripler for what he had done for him in California a few years before. Some time afterward this boy died. Dr. Tripler had known Gen. Sherman when a cadet at West Point.[157]

While in Newport Dr. Tripler became impressed with the magnitude of the impending civil conflict and tried to prepare for it. He had studied the Crimean War and other modern conflicts. He said in every well-contested battle one-third of the men are put *hors de combat.* In the Winter of 1860 to '61 he delivered a course of lectures on Military Surgery in the Cincinnati Medical College, foreseeing what was coming. The students were eager for this instruction. My husband through life was tried and irritated by the unfitness and unpreparedness of the general body of medical students. He deplored the admission into his chosen profession of so many young men of defective education, and such men had no chance to become Army Surgeons if they appeared before him while he was at the head of the Board of Examiners.

While in the field, the course Dr. Tripler adopted was to send soldiers North for treatment in hospitals whenever feasible, and there he wanted the volunteer surgeons to be put. He wanted the regular Army Surgeons with him in the field, for many of these he himself had trained.

Once Dr. Tripler was dining with Gen. Scott at his hotel. Gen. Scott had been ill and was under strict rule of diet prescribed by Dr. Tripler. Gen. Scott, who was a great gourmand, gave his order with much emphasis, calling for a most sumptuous repast. Dr. Tripler said

---

157. *Recollections*, 126-127. Sherman made no mention of the story in his memoirs. William Tecumseh Sherman Jr., nicknamed Willie, was born June 8, 1854, in San Francisco. He died of typhoid fever in October 1863 while with his father at the front.

nothing, but as soon as the General's plate was filled, said, "Waiter, remove the General's plate." Gen. Scott's face fairly flamed as the two looked at each other. Then he said, "You are right, Doctor. I am under your orders now." Had Gen. Scott taken another course Dr. Tripler would no longer have attended him and Gen. Scott knew this.

Dr. Tripler admired Scott in a certain way. He was the only big General we then had. He liked to talk of his own achievements. Officers, young and old, flattered him, and there was a good deal of what Dr. Tripler called "boot-licking." This was natural, because a Commanding General has such power to make under officers comfortable or uncomfortable. As an officer Dr. Tripler was himself always as firm as a rock. He obeyed an order on the instant and never sought an excuse. Yet Dr. Tripler would say, "Every one has some weak point. Perhaps most of us have points not so harmless as Scott's." For myself, I despised Gen. Scott and my husband and I used earnestly to disagree as to his character.[158]

IX. During the Civil War[159]

EHT's loyalty to country and support of her soldier husband is fully revealed in this section. They would be apart yet again, starting in April 1861 when CST was assigned to a post along the Potomac River not far from where she had grown up. Within four months, he would accept the duty of organizing the medical team that would care for the mammoth Army of the Potomac under Major-General George B. McClellan. The couple spent winter months of 1861-1862 together, he readying for what became the Peninsula Campaign, she helping him with his work and spending time on Capitol Hill as legislation progressed that would enable his promotion. Despite their efforts, matters would unfold far less positively than hoped.

---

158. *Recollections*, 127-129.
159. This portion of *Recollections*, 131-154, is presented in full.

In the Summer of 1861 Gen. Scott was manifestly breaking. A Virginian himself, the secession of his state and resignation of the many officers from the Army, caused him such distress as to make him really unfit for duty. As General of the Army he might have had the attendance of the Surgeon General or any other Medical Officer, but he always wanted Dr. Tripler to attend him. So, after coming to Washington from Patterson's command in the Shenandoah Valley, Dr. Tripler went each day to the boarding-place of Gen. Scott before his own active duties of the day. He tried to keep all disturbing influences from the General and to retain in him courage and hope. One day Dr. Tripler reached Gen. Scott's before he was dressed, and took up a morning paper to read while waiting. As he read he was suddenly conscious, by a passing shadow falling through the window which opened on the front portico, of a long, straggling figure. He thought to himself, "There comes another Army contractor: I will give him a good snub; it is an outrage for him to force his way to the General." (For even then Army contractors were notorious for their effrontery. And Dr. Tripler was annoyed that the outer guard had admitted this man to the house.) So, as he was conscious of his entrance into the parlour, Dr. Tripler, without turning or even lowering his paper, said quite sharply, "No, Sir, no, you cannot see Gen. Scott. It cannot be. He is ill and can see no one." And, then, he realized that all in the room were standing and in silence. He looked up and saw Abraham Lincoln. The President, of course, accepted the situation and withdrew. "But," Dr. Tripler said, "I just wanted the earth to swallow me. I wanted to crawl under the table." Afterward, Schuyler Hamilton, one of Scott's aides, told Lincoln of Dr. Tripler's distress and the President laughed heartily. Younger officers who had known Dr. Tripler to snub certain men who were officious or opinionated appreciated this story.

In the Winter of 1862 to '63, my Mother went to Washington to secure the appointment of Charles Bissell to West Point. While in the City she was invited to attend an entertainment by Hermann, the magician, at the White House. She at first thought she would not go, but finally was prevailed on to meet old Army friends, viz.:

Gen. Meigs[160], Gen. Andrew Porter[161] and Gen. Henry I. Hunt.[162] My Mother was talking with Pres. Lincoln (in the East Room, where the company was gathered) when Mrs. Lincoln entered. She had on a white silk dress and a garland of roses on her head—her favorite attire. My Mother said to the President, "How very young she is looking." Mr. Lincoln smiled and was evidently much pleased. The entertainment itself was amusing. Hermann asked for the loan of a watch from the company. Secretary Seward, after some little delay, handed his watch to Hermann, who proceeded at once to pound it vigorously in a mortar. It was shortly afterward found intact dangling from a curtain-pole in the room.

At the near prospect of Civil War I thought I would go mad. I would throw food into the grate. I wanted to die. Giving birth to three children in five years, together with Stuart's long illness, had affected me strangely.[163] When Dr. Tripler left Newport and went to the front I had to sell and pack and store and move. I spent the Summer of 1861 in Thorold, Canada, with my Mother and children.[164] In December, 1861, I went to Washington to join Dr. Tripler, and remained there till 25th March, 1862, when the Army of the Potomac moved to the Peninsula. I left all my children with my Mother in Canada. In Washington Dr. Tripler had one room only

---

160. Montgomery C. Meigs (1816-1892), Quartermaster-General of the Army during the War. The Triplers named a child after him.
161. A cousin of Mary Todd Lincoln, Porter (1820-1872) served as provost from 1861-1864.
162. Henry J. Hunt, as previously identified. Upon his death in 1889, he was buried in what is now known as the United States Soldiers' and Airmen's Home National Cemetery in Washington, D.C., near the President Lincoln and Soldiers' Home National Monument.
163. The three Newport babies were: Edgar Mackin Tripler, born November 13, 1856, died July 4, 1858; Edward Townsend Tripler, born March 17, 1859, died September 27, 1911; and Eunice Montgomery Meigs Tripler, born December 21, 1860, the day after South Carolina enacted its Ordinance of Secession. She married Louis A. Arthur in 1887 and died on September 25, 1911, two days before her brother.
164. Thorold is near St. Catharines, Ontario, west of Niagara Falls.

and very insufficient accommodation generally, and when my going on was mooted he wrote me that Washington was over-crowded and stricken with small-pox and had become one great military camp, but I replied that I "could roost on a lamp-post." Nearly every day in Washington I went to the Capitol to watch the progress of legislation which might affect my husband's rank[165]—and almost every evening I went to Dr. Tripler's office, where I soon found I could be of real help. He had to affix his signature to about eighty discharges of soldiers each day, and I could and did write his name on these papers so that no one could tell his signature from mine.

On Sundays Dr. Tripler would work till shortly before the time for the Celebration of the Holy Communion, which we would attend together, of course, and, after service, Dr. Tripler would return again to his office and to his work. There was little time for rest in those days. The Church we attended was St. John's, Dr. Smith Pyne the then Rector—the same I went to as a child. Dr. Tripler's office was in the "Seven Buildings" on Pennsylvania Avenue near 17th St.[166] He boarded only two doors away. His room was small and every appointment simple. He had not a large staff of workers. At the Capitol I tramped the pavement and the marble staircases with a heavy heart. I never went out evenings except to Dr. Tripler's office. One day Dr. Tripler was ill and I called in to attend him young Dr. Woodhull of the Army[167] who was caring for a small-pox patient near. I remember well the horse he rode, fully caparisoned and with a surgeon's beautiful

---

165. On December 10, a bill "to provide for the reorganization of the medical department of the Army," S. No. 97, was introduced by Senator Henry Wilson of Massachusetts. It was referred to the Committee on Military Affairs and the Militia, which Wilson chaired. *Congressional Globe*, 37th Congress, 2nd Session, Dec. 10, 1861, 37.
166. Located on the northwest corner of Pennsylvania Avenue NW at 19th Street, where McClellan had established the headquarters of the Army of the Potomac. The facades of two of the row houses still remain. It was but steps from the War Department building at Pennsylvania and 17th Street.
167. Alfred Alexander Woodhull (1837-1921), commissioned in September 1861 at age 24.

saddle-cloth. I next met this Dr. Woodhull in 1879 in San Francisco and he told me of the awe he felt as a young surgeon in coming into the presence of Dr. Tripler and that when I addressed him as "Charlie" he was entirely sure Divine retribution must overtake me.

I had one interview in person with Gen. McClellan, to whose staff my husband was attached as Chief Medical Director of the Army of the Potomac. I went alone and without my husband's knowledge to Gen. McClellan's house. At the door-step I met President Lincoln. He was in the famous suit of grey clothes. It was the early evening and the President had come to Gen. McClellan's for a conference. He and I stood together on the front step. As the door was opened the President stepped back to allow me to enter. No words passed between us. I noticed well his kindly face—with the deeply harassed look it bore.

I sent in my card to Gen. McClellan with a request to see him "for five minutes." When he appeared I told him at once my errand: "Dr. Tripler knows nothing of my coming, but he is suffering cruelly from insufficient rank. For example, every ambulance in the Army is subject to control by the Quartermaster's Department. Your Chief Quartermaster has the rank of General, while Dr. Tripler, with responsibility for 250,000 men, has the rank of Major." I said, "If you are suited with my husband give him the rank his duties require. If you are not suited with him, send him home." Gen. McClellan heard me in silence, looking at me calmly and gravely and said he would do all in his power to make Dr. Tripler's orders and suggestions effective. I said, "You are going to fight. Dr. Tripler asks hospital accommodations for 20,000 men and is laughed at. He is working with his hands tied. Every one else seems to have power to squander money." While I was talking with Gen. McClellan, his wife came to him and, after greeting me, inquired of him if Mrs. Smith (wife of Gen. "Baldy" Smith[168]) might depend on transportation between Washington and New York. From the projected move of the Army of the Potomac

---

168. William Farrar Smith (1824-1903), West Point Class of 1841, served as a Corps commander and reached the rank of Major-General.

people hardly knew what to expect and I took this question as showing Gen. McClellan's wife knew no more than any one else. I remember she had a knitting needle in her hand, and, as she spoke, she tapped her husband with it playfully on the shoulder.[169]

Later, in the field, Gen. McClellan gave to Dr. Tripler *carte blanche* to say "By order of Gen. McClellan," and, later still, commensurate rank was given to the Chief Medical Officer.[170]

The day of my interview with Gen. McClellan was the day of a great review of 20,000 reserve artillery under my Cousin, Gen. Henry I. Hunt. This I witnessed in company with Mrs. Heintzleman[171], and I never shall forget the sight of that host of men, their battery horses in full gallop advancing upon the very spot where we stood. Mrs. Heintzleman said, "Oh, let's get away quick." But a bugle sounded and the whole mass wheeled on the instant to the right and swept past in review.

At the solicitation and importunity of Mrs. Heintzleman I went to one White House reception by Mrs. Lincoln in the afternoon. I had no heart for such things then, but Mrs. Heintzleman prevailed on me. The wives of corps commanders were to assist in receiving, and so Mrs. Heintzleman and I stood behind Mrs. Lincoln in the line. Mrs. Lincoln was an ugly little woman. She wore a white silk dress, cut low in the neck, with a wreath of roses. I remember well when the wife of Gen. Emory was presented the word was added by the Marshal, "The great grand-daughter of Benjamin Franklin" (Mrs. Emory was formerly a Miss Bache of Philadelphia). To this Mrs. Lincoln's salutation

---

169. Mary Ellen Marcy (1836-1915) had married McClellan in 1860.
170. EHT's recollection of Dr. Tripler's authority is overstated, and he did not receive commensurate rank.
171. Margaret Stuart, wife of Samuel P. Heintzelman (1805-1880), West Point Class of 1826, who would serve as III Corps commander in the Peninsula Campaign and as Dr. Tripler's commanding officer in the Midwest. The Triplers had known them since their posting together at Newport Barracks. *Recollections*, 118.

was, "Do you keep your health?" It was so incongruous and ridiculous I could hardly control myself.[172]

Mrs. Lincoln had the reputation in Washington of a virago.[173] Certainly she did things that were not nice. One day Secretary Seward was going with the President to some affair of State. Mr. Lincoln came out of the White House and entered the carriage. From an upper window, Mrs. Lincoln cried out, "Stop, Abe, stop. Take these children with you" (Robert and Tad). "And," said Seward, "those children kicked my shins all through that ride." Mrs. Lincoln dismissed all the gardeners but one, and all the laundresses but one—saving, in this way, from the White House expenses for her own purse. So far as I know, she did one and only one kind act to a Union soldier. She one day ordered the White House gardener to take a bouquet of flowers to a poor soldier whom she saw resting on the curb-stone in front of the White House. Even then, I believe a drink of whiskey would have been better. New York merchants used to send garments to Mrs. Lincoln with letters asking the privilege to advertise that she would wear these things on certain occasions. It was all a great trial to the President. Yet he would turn it off …."

Several years after Mrs. Lincoln left the White House she offered her effects for sale. Robert Lincoln came out with a statement that his Mother had $60,000 in U.S. Bonds and a pension of $3,000 a year.

It was commonly reported and believed that at Mrs. Lincoln's instance, both the White House gardener and the White House coachman were commissioned as Lieutenants in the Army, and their pay, as officers, turned over to Mrs. Lincoln. Of course Mr. Lincoln knew nothing of this. When the Count de Paris and the Count de Chambord came to this country in 1862, Secretary Seward told

---

172. Since the order to appoint corps commanders was issued on March 8, 1862, this reception occurred thereafter. Her son "Willie" had died on February 20, and Mrs. Lincoln's grief did not abate. The wife of General William H. Emory (1811-1887) was Matilda Wilkins Bache (1819-1900), Franklin's great-granddaughter.
173. An ill-mannered female.

Mrs. Lincoln it was quite necessary to entertain them at dinner at the White House. Mrs. Lincoln said she was unwilling to make the arrangement unless the Government would meet the expense. But Secretary Seward was insistent it should be done. At the time a great quantity of manure had been delivered at the White House grounds to be spread afterwards upon the grass of the lawns. This Mrs. Lincoln managed to sell and from the proceeds provided for the entertainment which was afterwards known generally as "the manure dinner." When about to leave the White House in 1865 Mrs. Lincoln ordered all the silver of the table service to be packed up, preparatory to taking it with her. Of course she did not succeed in this.

When Gen. Heintzleman took command of his corps in Virginia we went one day to see him. A sentry was pacing at a considerable distance from his quarters. I asked "Why?" "To prevent any one coming near enough to hear the telegraph operator."

At Newport Dr. Tripler had operated on the daughter of Gen. and Mrs. Heintzleman for hip-joint disease, and successfully. They were most grateful.

As I watched Congress in session I remember seeing Henry Wilson of Massachusetts (Vice President in Grant's second term) look through his mail on his desk by simply tearing off the envelope and glancing at the signature. Without even pretending to read the letter in many cases he would tear it in two and throw it into his waste-basket. I took a violent dislike to him. I was watching the progress of a bill to make Medical Directors Generals of the Army.[174]

One day Dr. Bellows, the famous Unitarian Minister of New York City, and, at the time, far up in control of the "Sanitary Commission," came to Dr. Tripler and promised to make him Surgeon General if

---

174. The legislation, "An Act to reorganize and increase the Efficiency of the Medical Department of the Army," became law on April 16, 1862. The Surgeon-General would now hold the rank of Brigadier-General; his assistant and a medical Inspector-General of Hospitals were given the rank of Colonel. George P. Sanger ed., *The Statutes at Large*, Vol. XII (Boston: Little, Brown & Co., 1863), 378-379 (37th Congress, 1st Session, Act of April 16, 1862).

he would, in advance, give the Commission certain privileges. Dr. Tripler said, "No, Sir, I believe in regular succession both in Church and State."[175]

I remember some young surgeons who used to laugh at Dr. Tripler for taking some of their number twenty-five miles on horse-back in the morning on duty and again as far in the afternoon. Washington was full of small-pox that Winter. I remember a little German toy-shop that I visited with Mrs. Heintzleman. She said, "Oh, let's get out of this; I smell small-pox." The next morning the papers reported it there. Through the Winter my great fear was for Dr. Tripler, who could not sleep. He could not get Army surgeons to take the field. They would keep in the hospitals. A Dr. Keeney took a Saratoga trunk into the field. Dr. Tripler issued orders limiting the amount of baggage permitted to Medical Officers. There was no room in the trains for more. He said to a subordinate, "Here is all I have with me. If you find any of our officers with more than this put it out in the mud." And that is where Dr. Keeney's Saratoga trunk went.

When at last the Army moved into Virginia I remained for ten days or so in Washington. In company with Mrs. Heintzleman and a Mrs. Smith, wife of an Army surgeon, I went in an ambulance to visit Dr. Tripler. He was astounded at our advent and received us very coolly. "To think of my wife coming into Army life in the field." "But Mrs. Smith said to come." "If all the Mrs. Smiths in the world said it I would not expect you." I had brought out butter and a huge bowl of chicken-salad which I carried on my lap in the ambulance. But I could eat scarcely anything, for my husband was ashamed of me and I felt it. At last came the question, "Where shall we sleep?" Dr. Tripler said, "I have ordered the young surgeons to find quarters where they can for the night and you will take their cots." He added, "This is no place for a woman." We could not undress. In the camp all was mud and dirt. Early in the morning a soldier entered the tent where

---

175. Henry W. Bellows (1814-1882) served as president of the United States Sanitary Commission. The relationship between members of the Commission's board and Tripler proved complicated and less than optimal.

we were to make up the fire. It had before given me pain to think of the devastation of Virginia, but I saw those cedar posts burn without regret. Naturally, we started early on our return. I remember the principal furniture of Dr. Tripler's tent was a table, a stove and a horizontal pole across which hung his saddle.

In Washington I hardly ever went down town without seeing Gen. McDowell[176], obese, with protuberant stomach and a tight belt. He was in those days designing a new uniform for the Army and examining fabrics and colored plates. Meantime shoddy overcoats and garments were furnished the soldiers and blood money made by the Army contractors. Gen. Heintzleman used to say that every window curtain in Washington concealed two spies. He told me that President Lincoln was strangely obtuse to the danger of spies in the White House. On one occasion when a Council of War was being held there neither the doors nor windows of the apartment were closed until Gen. Heintzleman himself closed them. At the moment Gen. McClellan had been called on to disclose his plans for an advance on Richmond and was about to unfold them. Many thought that Lincoln himself ought to have realized the danger and guarded against it. Mrs. Lincoln was suspected of sending intelligence to her Brother in the Confederate service—stationed at this time but a short distance from Washington on the Virginia side of the Potomac.

When I left Washington for the North the crocuses were in bloom in the Capitol grounds. Two days later in Thorold my trunk had to be carried to the stable because the pathway to the house cut down through the snow was too narrow to admit its passage. The snow at the side of this pathway came up to my shoulders.

While the Army of the Potomac was at Yorktown, Sen. Zach. Chandler[177] visited the front, apparently under the impression that

---

176. Major-General Irwin McDowell (1818-1885), commander of Union troops in defeat at the Battle of First Bull Run, July 1861.
177. Zachariah Chandler (1813-1879), who held various public offices including U.S. Senator from Michigan during 1857-1875, was an outspoken critic of the institution of slavery on moral grounds. Martin J. Hershock, *The Para-*

his superior wisdom was badly needed by those in command. He was one of those who could not believe in the presence of an enemy unless a big battle was being fought every day. At the headquarters he said, "Where are the lines drawn? Where is this enemy anyway?" My Cousin, Gen. Henry I. Hunt, Chief of Artillery, turned to his Aide and said, "Capt. Bissell, take Mr. Chandler along the lines and draw the enemy's fire." This consisted in throwing a shell from almost every battery in position—and, in each case and most promptly, the return shot from the Confederates would plump right down on our line. Frightened? Poor Chandler was terrified almost to death. He wanted the firing to stop. But Charley Bissell said to him, "But, Sir, this cannot be. You know you wanted to be shown the enemy's exact position and I must obey my orders." And he took him along the entire line.

Dr. Tripler took an extra and brand new wig with him to wear at the glorious entry into Richmond—which all anticipated as the assured end of the Peninsular Campaign. But that wig was never worn.

As head of the Army of the Potomac Dr. Tripler had unbounded admiration and implicit confidence in McClellan. He thought McDowell too self-centred and overcome with vanity. He put no reliance in Pope[178], knowing him to be a falsifier and questioning his disinterestedness. He believed in the unstained patriotism of Burnside and his earnest and unselfish purpose. He thought Hooker a leader of courage, but deplored his being such an egotist. He knew Meade[179] as a topographical engineer, but hardly otherwise. The duties of engineer were far removed from those of an army surgeon. Of course Dr. Tripler knew Grant so long and so well in California that he thought,

---

dox of Progress: Economic Change, Individual Enterprise, and Political Culture in Michigan, 1837-1878 (Athens: Ohio University Press, 2003), 112. He rejected compromise with secessionists while maintaining the supremacy of federal law and the Union. Id. 162-163; John W. Quist ed., *Michigan's War: The Civil War in Documents* (Athens: Ohio University Press, 2019), 26.
178. Major-General John Pope (1822-1892), West Point Class of 1842, commander of the short-lived Army of Virginia in 1862.
179. Major-General George G. Meade (1815-1872), West Point Class of 1835, commander of the Army of the Potomac from 1863-1865.

in Grant's earlier campaigns, he was hardly a safe man to be entrusted with independent command on account of his personal habits. Yet he knew Grant had taken a good, though not brilliant, grade at West Point[180]—that he was unshaken in his loyalty to the Union—and knew enough not to talk too much about his military plans. He was a good deal surprised at Grant's earlier successes in the field, but, in his campaign of 1864, Dr. Tripler used to say, "I believe Grant will succeed." And no man anywhere rejoiced more truly than Dr. Tripler at his final triumph.

With Gen. Robert E. Lee Dr. Tripler had served in the Mexican War and for him he had a warm personal regard. I have sometimes thought the two had a sort of spiritual kinship. Lee had a beautiful Christian character, which was reflected in his attractive face. There was nothing of the "milk-sop" about him or Dr. Tripler either. Both were manly, independent Christians and neither of them, in any conceivable circumstances, could whine or squirm or indulge in any form of cant.

During the time of McClellan's Peninsular Campaign President Lincoln nominated Dr. Tripler as Surgeon General of the Army.[181] But political and personal influences prevented his confirmation by the Senate. At Harrison's Landing, Va., in July, 1862, Dr. Tripler was relieved and told he could have any duty outside the field. He chose to be Chief Surgeon in command of the Department of the Lakes, and came at once to Detroit. It is strange to think of the nature of the opposition that developed to Dr. Tripler. The Surgeon General was against him, for the rank of the two men was so nearly equal that their duties, especially the drawing of requisitions, had been conflicting and the experience had really been hard for both. Senator Howard was against Dr. Tripler. Zach. Chandler was against him. The Sanitary Commission was against him. The fact just then that he was on McClellan's staff weakened his cause. It is strange that a man like

---

180. Grant graduated 21st of 39 cadets in the West Point Class of 1843.
181. EHT's recollection is in error. Her husband was nominated for Inspector-General of Hospitals in the Army.

Chandler, whose life had been spent behind the counter of a shop, should presume to dictate what Dr. Tripler in his profession should or should not do. And there were positive reasons for his really befriending Dr. Tripler. My Brother-in-law, Mr. Bissell, years before, had, at Chandler's earnest solicitation, given him substantial help financially. Mr. Chandler was in straits at the time and did not wish to imperil his credit by effecting a loan. But Mr. Bissell borrowed the money he needed and lent it to him. This act saved Mr. Chandler from failure and business ruin. Dr. Farrand, himself a strong Republican, said the treatment accorded Dr. Tripler undoubtedly was the cause of his death. And Dr. Tripler had markedly befriended both Congressmen who now opposed him. When the Chandlers were about moving into their new home on Fort St. their daughter (afterward Mrs. Eugene Hale) was frightfully burned. Dr. Tripler attended her without fee. So, too, he was called to Mrs. Howard (being in the neighbourhood) when very suddenly taken ill and treated her successfully and gratuitously. Yet she afterward boasted that her husband had ruined Dr. Tripler. Of course my husband had intense desire to learn what charges could have been made against him. He wrote to Senator Howard to ask. The reply was very brief, stating simply that the proceedings of an Executive Session were never made public. Senator John Sherman afterward told Dr. Tripler that a soldier in Alexandria was promised his discharge if he would sign a complaint that the sick soldiers had to eat from the garbage of the camp to get food enough. "Will you vote to promote a man responsible for this?" And this infamous paper was read before the Senate and defeated him. Undoubtedly the men who represented the Sanitary Commission often found Dr. Tripler quick and brusque. When they were boring him he would say, "Excuse me, but I have my duties and men's lives are hanging on these moments." "But we have lint here for hospital use." "So have I, eleven tons of it on this steamer." "But here are night-shirts and pillows for the soldiers." "Well, what can men in camp do with such things? But leave them. They can clean their guns with them." Poor sewing women were scraping lint and Dr. Tripler said, "Why do this? We sent at once to Holland for all the lint we could need, and we have it." Then Dr. Tripler would not coddle newspaper correspondents. He would not talk for the sake of getting himself talked about. When Dr. Barnes[182] was made Surgeon General he wrote Dr. Tripler, "It was I or a civilian. I saved the office to the Medical Corps." In 1881 in Washington, Surgeon General Barnes told my daughter Eunice that no other man had ever done what her Father had to raise the spirit and tone of the Medical Corps. For years after Dr. Tripler's death it seemed to me I was walking about and being cared for by people who wanted to do for me for his sake.

During the Summer of 1862 my Mother was in Thorold, Canada, with my younger children. She had rented a small house for the season and was keeping her own home. On 4th July she put out the American flag. The rebel sympathizers and secessionists came up to the house, an excited, angry mob, demanding that the flag be taken down. There was a great uproar in the street. But my Mother stood firm and said the flag should stay. She threatened to throw boiling water on the crowd. Her Brother-in-law, George Kiefer, a magistrate, came to remonstrate with her. "Allie, you are wrong in this. I cannot protect you. If you do this you must take the consequences." "Consequences!" said my Mother, "They will take the consequences." And she got hot water and a dipper, and, from the roof of the front porch, she threw some water outward toward the crowd. The moment the steam was seen rising into the air the mob broke and ran. My Mother stood on guard till sundown—and had no dinner—fearing a sudden attack. And the flag floated all day on her "Castle."

My Mother had a keen sense of humor. And frequently visiting friends in Windsor and Amherstburg, Canada, she became disgusted at the self-importance and complacency of the Custom's Officers in the examining of baggage. On one occasion she took with her to Canada a hat-box needlessly large, and, on return by ferry to Detroit,

---

182. Joseph K. Barnes (1817-1883), Surgeon-General of the Army from 1864-1882.

she made a great pretense of confusion and reluctance at having to open it for inspection. "Must this really be? Is it actually necessary? Can you not take my word for it?" "No, Madam, it is absolutely necessary that everything herein be laid open before me." So my Mother finally produced the key and opened the box. Its contents did not fill one-fourth of the space, but she made the officer examine each article. "You know you said you must examine everything. Now this box contains powder. Unfortunately I am very vain and proud of my personal appearance. So this is a necessity to me. And here is a packet of court plaster. Of course you know how that is used. And this farther box contains the hidden secrets of my toilet." The man was greatly embarrassed, but my Mother forced him to look at everything.

In the Winter of 1862-'63, while living in our house on Woodward Avenue and Adelaide St., we were robbed of almost every article of family silver. My baby was worrying and I would have said in the morning that I had been up with him the whole night, but I must have slept while the burglary was in progress.[183] We found burnt matches all over the house, showing the men had dared to use a light. The few articles of plated ware, like a cake-basket and a pair of salt-cellars, had been tested by acid on the under side and left. All else was taken except one silver fork with which Dr. Tripler had eaten his baked potato in the study the evening before and one silver spoon with which I had mixed his toddy. We called on detectives at once, but nothing was ever recovered, nor was any one ever arrested for the crime. Very many of the things taken could never be replaced—but we must be philosophical in such experiences.[184]

---

183. Henry Hunt Tripler, their ninth and last child, had been born on Christmas Day 1862.
184. During this winter, Dr. Tripler prepared a full report on his service as Medical Director of the Army of the Potomac. He submitted it on February 7, 1863, from Detroit. See *The War of the Rebellion: A Compilation of the Official Records of the Union and Confederate Armies*, Series I (Washington: Government Printing Office, 1881, 1884), Volume V, 76-113, Volume XI, part I, 177-210. It is likely the document was aided by time in the home's study. The referenced intersection is now the site of Little Caesars Arena and the Woodward Place

In the Winter of 1863-'64, while Dr. Tripler was on duty as head of the Examining Board for Medical Officers in New York City, I was with him for some months. We boarded in Bleecker St. with a certain Dr. Mapes, a Professor of Chemistry, with whom my husband for long had a pleasant acquaintance. Dr. Mapes had taken a large house and had a number of boarders. One great advantage to us was the nearness to Dr. Tripler's office in the Army building. I remember that Dr. Mapes used to make out our monthly board bill to the "Temple of Friendship." We called one evening on the Grants at their hotel. They had two very small rooms. Gen. Grant made no splurge. Mrs. Grant had been suffering from cholera morbus and sent for me to come into her bed-room. She reminded me of Dr. Tripler's care of her in the earlier days and she said, "Now, Dr. Tripler must not come into this room." I said, "Certainly, he will not come here unless you send for him." She replied, "But I am afraid he may say to me, 'Mrs. Grant, you are ill and must not go out to-night. You must keep quiet just where you are.' But I have promised to go to the Opera and probably he won't let me." I answered, "But you can go to the Opera if you want to. Things have changed. You can trample on Dr. Tripler if you wish." But Mrs. Grant said, "But if Dr. Tripler forbids it, I wouldn't dare to go."[185]

In 1865 the Grants were in Detroit and a reception was given for them.[186] I was in evening dress. Late in the evening as I stood beside the Grants, Mrs. Grant nudged me with her elbow, school-girl fashion, as she said to her husband, "Now, General, here is Mrs. Tripler with a low-necked dress. I have a neck, too. But you don't let me wear such a dress." I said, "But you really ought to. Every woman is bound

---

townhomes.
185. An account of her New York sojourn is found in *The Personal Memoirs of Julia Dent Grant*, 130-131. See also Ishbel Ross, *The General's Wife: The Life of Mrs. Ulysses S. Grant* (New York: Dodd, Mead & Co., 1959), 173-174.
186. On August 12, 1865, the Grants arrived in Detroit for a stay at the Biddle Hotel, departing on August 15. *Detroit Daily Free Press*, Aug. 13, 1865, 1; John Y. Simon ed., *Papers of Ulysses S. Grant*, Vol. II (Carbondale: Southern Illinois University Press, 1967), 300-301.

to make the best appearance she can in observance of the proper customs of her time and station." I thought I would help her this much—for I was an older woman than she. Gen. Grant kept silent, uttering no single word—entirely impassive. He said in a moment, "Where is the Doctor?" I replied, "I think he has gone out for a smoke" (a fact). "Oh," said he, "and I have a pocket-full of cigars right here." He was plainly sorry they could not take their smoke together. I have reason to think that my words on this occasion had weight, for I understood that at like companies a little later Mrs. Grant wore rather more conventional attire. She certainly did, on the next occasion when I met her, which was in 1879 at a reception given by Gen. McDowell at Black Point in San Francisco Harbour.

At this reception one rather amusing incident occurred. A Priest of the Russian Church was standing in one of the rooms, with his hands folded and hidden in his flowing sleeves and his whole figure absolutely motionless. His face looked waxen. Not an eyelid nor a hair moved. I thought the object was a manikin, and said to Eunice, "This is a fine piece of art," and instinctively and without thought put out my hand and touched the figure—which, thereupon, moved off in a rather stately way, and to my own confusion.

During our stay in New York City, in 1864, Dr. Tripler and I called on Col. Robert Anderson (of Fort Sumter) and Mrs. Anderson and they several times visited us. Col. Anderson was a nervous wreck and showed it. His health was shattered by the fearful strain of his experiences in Charleston Harbour in the Spring of 1861, and he never again was strong.

There seemed to be a very moving hero-worship in the South, especially on the part of the women, during the Civil War. This I account for from the fact, as I think it to be, that the Southern leaders were, speaking generally, more tender and chivalrous than those of the North. Their ideals were not so mercenary. Their breeding had been different.[187]

---

187. EHT's opinion appears to have succumbed to the "Lost Cause" narrative.

Correspondence she received from a cousin in July 1863 addressed to "My dear Eunice," reveals her keen interest in the conduct of the Civil War. Responding to two letters from her, Henry J. Hunt replied: "Your last one just poured coals of fire on my head." Eunice had been "flattened out because we didn't bag Lee" during the recent campaign. She also inquired how George G. Meade "came to be appointed" to command the Union side. Although the Army of Northern Virginia had suffered defeat during the Battle of Gettysburg on July 1-3, it had been permitted to escape across the Potomac into Virginia. Hunt defended the performance of the Army of the Potomac, but relevant to this study are the extent of detail and lack of condescension in his explanation. It seems likely the two had a history of such exchanges, that he regarded Eunice as capable of comprehending the complexity of military matters in major conflicts, and that she did not hesitate to question and challenge strategy and tactics. She was obviously knowledgeable and intensely engaged.

X. Dr. Tripler's Death[188]

Looking back a third of a century after the demise of her husband, EHT's loyalty to his memory and reputation proves faithful. She appears as a full partner of the work he performed from the day of their 25-year marriage.

After his retirement from the field, Dr. Tripler's duties as Chief Surgeon of the Department of the Lakes were in Detroit, Columbus and Cincinnati, as headquarters was moved from time to time.[189] The last home of Dr. Tripler was on Lafayette Avenue near 3d St.[190] My Husband's illness began in the Spring of 1866, when trouble developed

---

188. This portion of *Recollections*, 155-164, is presented in full.
189. He was a prime mover beginning in 1863 behind the establishment of a soldiers' hospital in Detroit known as Harper Hospital. Lanman, 217; John Robertson, *Michigan in the War* (Lansing: W.S. George & Co., 1882), 115-116.
190. The site today of the former *Detroit News* and WWJ Radio buildings. During EHT's life in Detroit, the *Detroit Evening News* offices were at Shelby and Larned streets.

in the right ear. Three small glands on the side of the face became implicated, one after another. He suffered no pain till seven months before his death, when the malignant character of the disease became apparent.

While lying ill in the Summer of 1866 Dr. Tripler received a call from Gen. Grant ("swinging round the circle" with President Johnson) and Gen. Rawlins[191] of his personal staff and Gen. Barnes, the Surgeon General. The party came by boat to Detroit from Cleveland. They came to our house shortly after breakfast. Gen. Rawlins (whom Dr. Tripler knew but slightly) remained downstairs and talked very pleasantly with my Mother. Gen. Grant and Surgeon General Barnes went up to Dr. Tripler's room. Gen. Barnes threw himself on his knees at the bedside and embraced Dr. Tripler—told him much about the Army, why he himself had accepted the Surgeon-Generalship, viz., to keep out some civilian, who otherwise would have had it, and so save it to the Medical Corps. The Sanitary Commission was making and unmaking everything. The Commission had put Hammond into the Surgeon-Generalship, who had accepted the bargain Dr. Tripler declined—and he had been cashiered.[192] During all this talk Gen. Grant scarcely spoke. Downstairs, however, he talked with my Mother rather more freely. She asked him, among other things, why there was a fort at Yuma. (Charles Bissell had been stationed there.) In reply Gen. Grant said, "Nobody knows, Mrs. Hunt, for the reason that nobody has ever been able to find out."

The attention of this call from the General of the Army and the Surgeon General was very gratifying to Dr. Tripler. He regarded it as a personal testimony that his own character and services were esteemed far above the indication by the rank accorded him.

One afternoon in the Summer of 1866 Bishop McCoskry called to see Dr. Tripler. I chanced to be away when he came, but returned home as the Bishop closed his call and met him coming down the

---

191. John A. Rawlins (1831-1869), staff officer to Grant and close associate.
192. EHT's recollections here do not track the historical record precisely.

stairs. He said, "Mrs. Tripler, I called to teach your husband, but I find he has taught me." He showed much emotion.

The first week in October, 1866, Dr. Tripler went on to Cincinnati to have Dr. Blackman examine him. Of course I accompanied him. Death came finally (October 20th) and released him from his anguish.

My Cousin, Henry Hazard, insisted on accompanying me with the body to Detroit. Dr. Freyer and Mr. Radcliffe met us in Toledo. At Newport, before starting, Mrs. Swords brought me her bonnet and black veil. "You must use these. The veil will be a great relief and protection." And so I found it on the journey, for I was weeping much.

Dr. Tripler's funeral took place 22d October, 1866, from St. John's Church, Detroit. Nearly all the Clergy of the city were present. It was a military funeral. Dr. Pitcher was in charge.[193] The artillery and infantry from Fort Wayne were in the procession. Four guns were dragged to Elmwood Cemetery.[194] Non-commissioned officers bore the body. Eight Army Officers were the pall-bearers—at their head Gen. Joe Hooker. From Columbus Gen. Hooker had telegraphed to know about the arrangements and who were to be pall-bearers. He was told. He said, "But where am I to be? Am not I to be pall-bearer for my friend?" Some one said, "But, Gen. Hooker, you are too infirm to serve so." "Then," said he, "I will ride in my carriage beside the hearse and act as bearer in that way." And this he did.

Dr. Tripler's death was announced to the Army by a General Order (of which I have a copy—No. 89). Gen. Hunt wrote me this was an unusual thing and a great honor to the Medical Department, which was put into mourning for three months.[195]

In the Surgeon General's report of Dr. Tripler's death to the Adjutant General he uses these words concerning Dr. Tripler: "His

---

193. Zina Pitcher (1797-1872) served on the Army medical staff before becoming Mayor of Detroit, Regent of the University of Michigan, and President of the American Medical Association, among other offices he held.
194. Historic Elmwood Cemetery in on the east side of the city of Detroit at East Lafayette Street and Robert Bradby Drive.
195. See Appendix.

skillful administration and conscientious discharge of duty have been rewarded by three brevets for 'faithful and meritorious services.' The Medical Corps possesses, in his distinguished career, a bright example of the union of professional attainments, with the military zeal and pride of an officer and those qualities which mark the Christian gentleman."

The marble monument over my husband's grave was erected by the Medical Corps of the Army. It was executed in Buffalo, N.Y., and its cost was $800. Major Farquhar[196] made the drawing of the wreath of laurel cut upon the Cross in relief. I had a most interesting correspondence with Dr. Satterlee[197] in regard to the project. The Surgeon General issued a circular to the Medical Corps on the matter. Subscriptions were limited in amount. Surgeons were not to give over $10 each and Assistant Surgeons not over $5. A very large proportion gave. Dr. Satterlee afterward sent me all the letters received. Many of them were most gratifying to me in their tone. One wrote he feared no suitable monument could be erected for such a sum and requested he might be called on again. Another wrote expressing his gratitude for Dr. Tripler's example and reputation, which, he said, were enough to stimulate himself and all other young surgeons to attain their highest ideal. This man had no personal acquaintance with Dr. Tripler.

Bishop Armitage[198] once sent me (from Milwaukee) a copy of the "Pacific Churchman" with a letter from Bishop Kip of California, then East, in which he told of being in Detroit and driving with some friends through Elmwood Cemetery. He was attracted toward a certain monument and left the carriage to inspect it. It was the monument to Dr. Tripler—a most remarkable coincidence—as the Bishop said "The only stone among all those thousands raised in memory of

---

196. Francis U. Farquhar (1838-1883), West Point Class of 1861 (June), had served in the Peninsula Campaign and in the Army Corps of Engineers.
197. Richard S. Satterlee (1798-1880) served at the Detroit Barracks and during the Civil War as a Medical Purveyor.
198. William E. Armitage (1830-1873) was an Episcopal Church bishop in Wisconsin.

one I knew and loved." A large portrait of Dr. Tripler, done in India ink, hung for many years in the main hall of the old Army Medical Museum in Washington surrounded by much smaller pictures of past Surgeon Generals—a recognition of my husband's character and career very gratifying to me. Through the kindness of Gen. E.O.C. Ord, a duplicate of this picture, handsomely framed, was sent me, as a gift from the Medical Corps.

Dr. Tripler wrote his Manual for recruiting officers in 1858 while we were at Newport.[199] He did not copyright the book because he meant to add to it. Of the first edition the Government took 750 copies and paid him a royalty of $350 thus formally recognizing his ownership. During the Civil War the Government issued many thousands of copies to the recruiting stations. Immediately on Dr. Tripler's death I applied for a pension and got one of $25 per month. In a year or so I applied for reimbursement for the Government's use of the Manual. I wrote to Senator John Sherman.[200] He replied that he would talk with Senator Edmunds[201] about my claim. It seems that Senator Edmunds opposed it on the ground that existing laws were sufficient and thus my case became hopeless. Two or three years later Congressman Lord[202] introduced in Congress a bill for my direct compensation for the Government's use of the work. My case, in its presentation, was strengthened by letters commendatory of the Manual and of the justice of my claim from Gen. McClellan (three in number) Gen.

---

199. The precise title of this volume is: *Manual of the Medical Officer of the Army of the United States, Part I, Recruiting and the Inspection of Recruits, by Charles S. Tripler, M.D., Surgeon U.S.A.; Fellow of the College of Physicians and Surgeons of the University of the State of New York* (Cincinnati: Wrightson & Co., 1858). In 1866, a second edition was issued by the Government Printing Office.
200. John Sherman (1823-1900) was U.S. Senator from Ohio 1861-1877 and 1881-1897. He was brother to William T. Sherman.
201. George F. Edmunds (1828-1919) was U.S. Senator from Vermont 1866-1891.
202. Henry W. Lord (1821-1891) was a Member of the U.S. House of Representatives from the 1st district of Michigan from March 4, 1881 to March 3, 1883.

W.T. Sherman, Gen. Henry I. Hunt, Gen. W.S. Rosecrans[203], Gen. E.D. Townsend, Surgeon Gen. Barnes, Adjutant Gen. Drum[204]. All these letters were finally lost to me in the Congressional Committees. Dr. Moore, Surgeon General, in a letter commending the book and expressing the hope that at least $10,000 would be allowed me for it, used these words, "It was of inestimable value, coming as it did at exactly the right time and in the day of our great need."[205] The first form of the bill was to grant me $10,000. The second bill was to pay me one-third of a cent for each copy used; another bill a fraction of a cent for each man enlisted by use of the Manual (about 3,000,000). Finally, the bill was fixed at $3,000 in which form it was for years before Congress at each session. Senator Palmer[206] told me $2,500 was the utmost sum he could get the Senate Military Committee favorably to consider. But, later, Senator McMillan[207] got it through the Senate Committee and it passed the Senate itself at six sessions at $3,000 only to be hung up on the calendar of the House and never get to its final stage in that branch of Congress. Congressman Levi T. Griffin[208] was the only Michigan Congressman who returned to me the papers committed to him. After my many years of failure and deferred hope it was almost against my wish—certainly without any expectation of success on my own part—that the bill, after my removal to Nebraska,

---

203. William S. Rosecrans (1819-1898) served as Major-General in the Union Army.
204. Richard C. Drum (1825-1909) served as Adjutant-General in the Army from 1880-1889.
205. John Moore (1826-1907) served as the Army Surgeon-General from 1886-1890.
206. Thomas W. Palmer (1830-1913) was U.S. Senator from Michigan from 1883-1889.
207. James McMillan (1838-1902) was U.S. Senator from Michigan from 1889-1902.
208. Levi T. Griffin (1837-1906) a Member of the U.S. House of Representatives from the 1st congressional district from December 4, 1893 to March 3, 1895. The *Detroit Free Press* hailed his effort, calling the bill "simply an act of justice to a worthy woman." Feb. 16, 1894, p. 1.

was again introduced in January, 1906. Senator E.J. Burkett[209] introduced it in the Senate and proved my devoted and faithful friend in securing its passage by that body—while Congressman G.W. Norris[210] was the most efficient and successful advocate of my cause in the House—where, really to my great surprise, the bill was finally passed 19th January, 1907—the anniversary of my husband's birth. I feel very grateful to my many friends who wrote to various Congressmen in my behalf.[211]

Once, at a recruiting station, Dr. Tripler was engaged in examining a man before a certain surgeon to exemplify his own methods of examination prescribed in his manual. The man under examination was extremely anxious to enter the army and was, of course, stripped and on all fours for the purpose of certain measurements and certain motions. As he ended his examination, Dr. Tripler turned to the desk to make a record and, in a moment, the surgeon present said to him in a low tone "Doctor, the recruit is still in the same position." Dr. Tripler glanced over his shoulder and seeing the man yet on all fours said to him simply "Jump up, now." This order the man interpreted literally, and, in a moment, began to leap into the air by a series of astonishing capers. There were some students present who were convulsed with laughter but Dr. Tripler felt rather confused by it.

Dr. Tripler wrote less than he studied but his stores of knowledge were always at the service of his professional friends in civil life, who had less time than himself to give to books. So far as I know he printed but these:

- Remarks on Delirium Tremens, 1827, being his graduating Thesis, published by request.[212]

---

209. Elmer J. Burkett (1867-1935) served in both the U.S. House of Representatives and U.S. Senate (1905-1911) from Nebraska.
210. George W. Norris (1861-1944) represented Nebraska in the U.S. House of Representatives from 1903 until 1913.
211. See Appendix for legislative history regarding EHT's efforts to secure this royalty payment.
212. The full title and detail: *Remarks on Delirium Tremens, or the Irritative Fever of Drunkenness: An Inaugural Dissertation, Submitted to the*

- A Treatise on the Duties of Physicians in regard to popular Delusions.[213]
- A Treatise on the nature, cause and treatment of Scurvy.[214]
- Manual for the Medical Officers of the Army of the United States. Part I. Recruiting and the inspection of Recruits. 1858.
- Handbook for the Military Surgeon, 1861.[215]

These last two were incomplete, the latter on account of his going to the field at the beginning of the Rebellion and the former being only the first part of the work which he hoped that he might live to complete to his own satisfaction.

Dr. Tripler felt deeply whenever he observed a soldier in garrison doing small duties in connection with an officer's home, done by servants elsewhere, like watching the children, or dragging a baby-carriage. My husband said these things were demoralizing to the soldier himself and degrading to the service and ought to be prohibited. The gratuity given by the officers for such work was not properly an element in the case.

My husband, in the fifties, made a will in which he solemnly charged me never to permit a child of ours "To enter a schismatical

---

Examination of the Faculty of the College of Physicians and Surgeons of the University of the State of New York (New York: J. Seymour, [April 3,] 1827), a 22-page pamphlet. It was republished in 1857 by Tripler with an introductory paragraph.

213. *The Duties of Physicians in Relation to Popular Medical Delusions: An Address Delivered Before the Covington and Newport Medical Society, June 14, 1859* (Covington: S.G. Cobb, 1859).

214. *The Causes, Nature, and Treatment of Scurvy: A Paper Read Before the Covington and Newport (Ky.) Medical Society* (n.p., ca. 1858).

215. EHT did not include the following: first, an excerpt from a report of Surgeon Tripler from Detroit Barracks, found on page 46, and the full text of a "report by Surgeon Charles S. Tripler" from San Francisco, California, dated September 14, 1852, found on pages 454-458, in *Statistical Report on the Sickness and Mortality in the Army of the United States, Compiled from the Records of the Surgeon General's Office, Embracing a Period of Sixteen Years, from January, 1839, to January 1855*, Senate Exec. Doc. No. 96, 34th Congress, 1st Session (Washington: A.O.P. Nicholson, 1856).

place of worship." Two months before he died he wrote another will in which no such direction appeared for he said it now seemed to him as being a reflection against me in some sort—"as either not knowing or not willing to do the right thing without instruction" from him.

Dr. Tripler entered the Military Order of the Loyal Legion at its inception, becoming a member of the first Commandery—that of Pennsylvania. His insignia came to me from Headquarters some time after his death.[216]

XI. A Few General Remarks[217]

This final section collects a number of vignettes that were too interesting to leave out of the memoir. Much of it adds details to her husband's life and career, but among those pertaining only to the author is the recognition of having known seven commanding Generals of the U.S. Army. Some personal proverbs provide a measure of the wisdom gained during nearly eighty-eight orbits around the sun, concluding with an avowal of the faith that carried Eunice Hunt Tripler through the vagaries of an astonishing life.

During his term in the White House President Hayes[218] visited Detroit. At a reception at Gov. Baldwin's[219], my Mother told the President she had danced with Ex-President Monroe[220] at the Inaugural Ball of John Quincy Adams in 1825 and had met at some time every man who had held the office of President since. This announcement was received by Mr. Hayes with a good deal of interest—and it livened things up—for the reception had been heavy and rather dull.

---

216. *Recollections*, 155-164.
217. This portion of *Recollections*, 165-176, is presented in full.
218. Rutherford B. Hayes (1822-1893), Brevet Major-General and 19th President of the United States (1877-1881). On a Midwest tour, he gave a speech in Detroit on September 18, 1879.
219. Henry P. Baldwin (1814-1892), Governor of Michigan from 1869-1873, lived in Detroit.
220. James Monroe (1758-1831), 5th President of the United States.

A Capt. Jamieson, already married three times, was on the point of taking his fourth wife. He came to Dr. Tripler to learn the Order of the Marriage Service in the Prayer Book, for he said, seriously and very solemnly, "I have generally been married by a Presbyterian."

A story much enjoyed by Gen. Grant and often told by Dr. Tripler was this. A soldier who had been stationed sometime at Fort Yuma died. A circle of Spiritualists later claimed to have communicated with him. He said he was getting on pretty well but he really wanted his heavy overcoat. He was asked, "Why?" He replied, "Well, after a man has been at Fort Yuma for a while, Hell is an awfully cold place to live in."

I have known personally seven Commanding Generals of the Army, viz.: Brown, Mc-Comb, Scott, McClellan, Grant, Sherman and Sheridan.[221] My acquaintance with Gen. Sheridan was of the slightest. The mother of Mrs. Sheridan was the adopted daughter of Col. (afterward Gen.) Whistler of the old Army.[222] On account of my acquaintance with Gen. Whistler I once called on Mrs. Sheridan at the Russell House, Detroit[223]. Gen. Sheridan came into the room and I, of course, met him. After he had gone Mrs. Sheridan spoke of the personal interest and magnetism her husband every where excited. She contrasted him in this regard with Gen. Grant and his stolidity. She told me Mrs. Grant once said to her that, on one occasion in public, if she could have gotten near her husband she would have stuck a pin into him to wake him up.

Gen. Halleck[224] in command of our Armies from July, 1862, to March, 1864, I never knew—though he and Dr. Tripler had served together and were personal friends.

It almost startles me, to try to realize the unbounded interest, Dr.

---

221. Philip H. Sheridan (1831-1888), Major-General of the Union Army, served as General of the Army from 1883 until his death.
222. Joseph N.G. Whistler (1822-1899), West Point Class of 1846, Brevet Brigadier-General in the Union Army,
223. A prestigious hotel on the Campus Martius.
224. Henry W. Halleck (1815-1872), Major-General in the Union Army.

Tripler, if alive, would be showing in the modern advance of medicine and surgery, especially the latter. He used to talk to the younger surgeons in the army to impress upon them the value of study—and the value of the habit of study. He told them that whenever they were stationed in or near large cities their opportunities were exceptional for making advance in professional attainments.

Dr. Tripler's attention was once called to the case of a poor man in Ypsilanti, Michigan, who had been injured by a railway train. As I remember it, both his legs and arms were broken and one thigh bone, several ribs and both collar bones. He had been given up to die when Dr. Tripler took him in charge, making the journey from Detroit to Ypsilanti, several times a week, until his complete recovery. The poor fellow's gratitude was moving. He was a cabinet-maker and taught his art to Dr. Tripler—who made for me, with his own hands, a stand and several light chairs. The great element in this recovery was the man's hope and good cheer.

After his marriage, Dr. Tripler's Army service was as follows:

1841-1846: Detroit.
1846-1849: Mexico.
1850-1852: Detroit and Fort Gratiot.
1852-1856: California.
1856-1861: Newport Barracks.
1861-1862: Field.
1862-1866: Department of the Lakes.

Dr. Tripler was graduated as M.D. from the College of Physicians and Surgeons (Medical Department of Columbia College, New York) 27th March, 1827.

He was appointed Assistant Surgeon in the Army 30th October, 1830, his commission being signed 15th March, 1831, by Andrew Jackson.[225]

---

225. According to the *Senate Executive Journal* of December 17, 1830, pages

He was appointed Surgeon 7th July, 1838, his commission being signed 10th July, 1838, by Martin Van Buren.[226]

He received the honorary degree of M.A. from Columbia College, New York, 26th June, 1860. He was appointed Colonel by Brevet 29th November, 1864, his commission being signed 23d March, 1865, by Abraham Lincoln.[227]

He was appointed Brigadier General by Brevet 13th March, 1865, his commission being signed 7th March, 1867, by Andrew Johnson.[228]

In the Summer of 1865 I was in Columbus, Ohio, with Dr. Tripler, and we were guests at the hotel where Gen. Rosecrans stayed. At table one day I remarked that it seemed to me Gen. McClellan was rather a taciturn man. "Taciturn," said he, "Tacit urn, empty urn." No love was lost, apparently, between these two.[229]

130, 132, President Jackson nominated for appointment as assistant surgeon in the U.S. Army, to date from October 30, 1830, "Charles I. Triplett, N.Y."; and on February 28, 1831, page 166, the Senate acted to confirm the nomination; on July 7, 1838, pages 145, 152, President Van Buren nominated Tripler for promotion to surgeon on that date; and on that same day, page 153, the Senate acted to confirm the nomination.

226. According to the *Senate Executive Journal* of July 7, 1838, pages 145, 152, President Van Buren nominated Tripler for promotion to surgeon on that date; and on that same day, page 153, the Senate acted to confirm the nomination.

227. According to the *Senate Executive Journal* of January 6, 1865, pages 32-33, President Lincoln nominated Tripler for a brevet as colonel on December 12, 1864, to date from November 29, 1864, and on February, 20, 1865, page 177, the Senate acted to confirm the nomination.

228. According to the *Senate Executive Journal* of December 14, 1866, page 33, President Johnson approved a post-mortem nomination of Tripler on December 11, 1866, to be brigadier-general by brevet "for faithful and meritorious services during the war, to date from March 13, 1865." The nomination was reported favorably (pages 237-238) and confirmed on February 23, 1867 (page 246), recalled by the Senate on February 25 (page 268), returned by the President on March 1 (page 283), reconsidered and recommitted to committee on March 2 (page 328), reported and confirmed on March 2 (page 337).

229. In 1870, EHT remained in Detroit and was recorded as a "widow keeping house." Also in the residence were Charles, age 24, and four other children ages 7 to 18 (pp. 57-58, 1st Ward, City of Detroit). The 1880 U.S. Census recorded her in Detroit, widowed and "Keeping house." Also recorded: Eunice, 19, "at home," Henry, 17, "RR clerk," Edward, 21, "wks in car shop" (p. 18,

I actually ache when I think of the world's scientific advance and all the problems inventors are now solving. It seems to me very great folly to put human life so in peril to reach the highest speed attainable by rail or automobile. Yet I sympathise with the toil and anxiety of these men and often wonder if the human race is better off in the long run. I can see no sign it is any happier—but rather the contrary. The world moves too fast in these days. It seems to me to lack even a tranquil enjoyment of its very pleasures.

I remember once, at about the age of seven or eight years, examining the veining and structure of a small leaf—and being so impressed by the evident plan and purpose of its Maker that I shed tears.

At the time of the "Old Catholic" conference at Bonn, Germany, under the leadership of Pere Hyacinthe, I was greatly scandalized by the press accounts of those good men discussing the weightiest and most spiritual subjects with great cans of beer at their elbows and in an atmosphere blue with tobacco smoke.

The impertinences of the modern press are simply intolerable. I often read what I think would abundantly justify the use of a horsewhip on the writer.

In Army command I believe the inexperience and enthusiasm of youth are better than the natural conservatism and imbecility of old age.

Honest workmanship is at a discount in these days. Very few men seem willing to do what is right because simply it is right.

The disregard of human life in modern methods of travel is to me most strange. The feverish rush and hurry and crowding—the indifference to another's rights, the inattention to another's comfort—are hard for me to reconcile with my old ideas of the sanctity of the individual. And it seems to me that the saving of time we effect is almost pitiful—when so compared with its true cost.

Dr. Tripler once deliberately changed his penmanship for

---

supervisor district 1, enumeration district 270). Their address was 86 Howard Street, very near to the city center.

me—altering it to make it more legible. This involved much time spent in practice. Few persons would do so much for another now, as I feel—and yet, the very basis of true courtesy is the comfort of others.

I am actually frightened when I see by the newspapers the cheapening and insecurity of life in modern days. When I was a child if we heard of a murder what made the story unspeakably horrible was the universal feeling that we should presently hear of someone's being hung for the crime. This fear or expectation of punishment does not seem now to exist—and it is to this cause I largely attribute our present conditions.

That men should speak on public questions with personal disinterestedness and act on them with simple honesty and an eye to the general good seems to-day to be, as the philosophers say, "the unthinkable." Yet in all these modern movements a Hand higher than that of man is to be seen and it is often not difficult to perceive its guiding.

I feel that my life, especially in its latter part, has been even wonderfully marked by the kindnesses done me. It seems again and again as though I had but stretched forth my hand to have it filled. And so much has been done for me in a beautifully deferential way. My tastes have been consulted. "Would not you like this or that?"

The longest time Dr. Tripler and I were together without break was the five years in Newport Barracks, Kentucky, 1856-'61. We always hoped in old age to have all our children about us, with no more anxieties nor separations. It has been otherwise ordered.

I consider my removal from the Lake region to Nebraska in 1900 as one of the greatest physical blessings in my old age. My obstinate bronchitis of more than twenty-five years' standing, it was plainly beyond the art of man to cure, and, at times, it had given me the greatest distress, but in less than two months after the move, every trace of it had disappeared, as also had the rheumatic pains from which I had long suffered. I have no active malady. I feel only the discomfort of increasing weakness. As they turn now the wheels make friction—for the machine is running down. (December, 1908.)[230]

In middle life my height was 5 feet 2 inches. My weight at 38 or 39 years of age was 127 lbs. It was never that after Dr. Tripler's death.

Once I was walking with Dr. Tripler in the old-fashioned way, arm in arm, on Jefferson Avenue, Detroit. I was suddenly conscious of his being in deep emotion. I looked up and saw his eyes were filled with tears and he presently recited softly and reverently the opening words of the old hymn:

> *"When all Thy mercies, O my God,*
> *My rising soul surveys,*
> *Transported with the view, I'm lost*
> *In wonder, love and praise."*[231]

And he said he did not deserve me nor the blessings of his home. He had a far too exalted opinion of my capabilities and character generally.

In old age it is surprising how we get accustomed to living. When my husband died I felt I must go too. I was in haste for the change. But the thought and desire passed. Now, in my old age and with love of life still strong upon me, I feel otherwise. In view of all the changes I have lived through I often feel as though I belonged to a former age of the world. With my mind all is now clear and I accept the fact of the approaching end of my life. I look on my hands and see they are old. I am old. Yet we cannot now realize what life is without the body. But that we shall be cared for of the Good Father I know.[232]

---

230. EHT's Detroit physician was Dr. Edwin Stanton Sherrill (1854-1945), graduate of the University of Michigan and the College of Physicians and Surgeons of New York, and for whom a public school on Garden Street near Livernois was named to honor his service in Detroit. Of his patient, he wrote: "Her frail body was the abode of an appealing spirit." *Detroit Medical News*, 1945, 6.
231. Written by Joseph Addison (1672-1719).
232. *Recollections*, 165-173.

★ ★ ★

Obituary

From the Detroit "News" of Thursday, 31 March, 1910.

Mrs. Eunice Tripler, who was this afternoon buried in Elmwood cemetery, died on Monday last at St. Stephen's rectory, Grand Island, Neb., where she had made her home for the last ten years with her daughter, Mrs. L.A. Arthur.

She was long a resident of Detroit and was a woman of an interesting personal history. She was born in Washington, D.C, in 1822, being the daughter of Capt. Thomas Hunt, U. S. Army, and her education was prosecuted in that city with rather exceptional advantages for so early a day. In 1836 her father removed to Detroit and her education was completed here and in a Church school in Utica, N.Y.

In 1841 she was married to Surgeon Charles S. Tripler of the regular Army. Dr. Tripler served in the Seminole and Mexican wars and in the Civil War as first Medical Director of the Army of the Potomac on the staff of Gen. McClellan. Dr. Tripler died in 1866, leaving an enviable record for professional attainment and for integrity and uprightness in every relation of life. Their children were nine in number, of whom four survive: Mrs. E.C. Hutchinson, of San Francisco; Edward T. Tripler of this city; Mrs. Louis A. Arthur of Grand Island, Neb., and H.H. Tripler, of Tacoma, Wash.

Among the earliest recollections of Mrs. Tripler was that of Gen. Lafayette during his visit to this country in the years 1826-7 and his long stay in Washington, where he was a frequent visitor at her father's house.

The winter of 1861-62 Mrs. Tripler passed in Washington with her husband, and she had a fund of pleasant anecdote[s] concerning President and Mrs. Lincoln and Washington life at that stirring time. She knew well, one might say, intimately, seven commanding Generals of the Army, from Gen. Alexander McComb down to and including Gen. Philip H. Sheridan.

With Mrs. Tripler the powers of a mind of much more than ordinary grasp had been developed by a course of liberal reading and study, and she was wont to express herself on topics of the day in quite an original fashion and with a brightness and sense of humor which made her conversation most enjoyable to all who knew her.

Mrs. Tripler was a sincere and faithful Christian and a devoted and self-sacrificing wife and mother, and to all connected with her by the ties of kinship or in the wider circle of mere social acquaintance she has left the witness of a singularly pure and devout life.[233]

★ ★ ★

---

233. *Recollections*, 175-176.

Historic Sites

I. Eunice's Detroit Homes
- Congress and Shelby streets, southeast corner
- "The Parsonage" on Woodbridge Street back of Christ Church
- Congress Street, two doors west of Shelby Street
- Jefferson Avenue at Brush Street, near the Biddle House hotel
- on the River Road at about 13th Street
- corner of Cass and Fort
- Jefferson Avenue/ home on Fort Street (during the California posting)
- Woodward Avenue and Adelaide Street
- Lafayette Avenue near Third Street

II. Structures of the Era

A number of buildings in Detroit date from the period when the Tripler family lived there together before the surgeon's death. Among these are:
- Charles Trowbridge house, 1380 E. Jefferson Ave. (1826; oldest known in the city)
- James Smith farmhouse, 2015 Clements St. (ca. 1830-50)
- U.S. & Julia D. Grant house, at the corner of Wilkins and Orleans streets as part the Eastern Market district (1837)
- Christopher Moross house, 1460 E. Jefferson Ave. (1843-48)
- Judge Solomon Sibley house, 976 E. Jefferson Ave. (1848)

- Saints Peter & Paul Church, 629 E. Jefferson Ave. (1848)
- Worker's row house, 1430 Sixth St. (1849)
- Old Mariners' Church, 170 E. Jefferson Ave. (originally, foot of Woodward) (1849)
- Beaubien/Charles Trombly house, 553 E. Jefferson Ave. (1851)
- John Purdon house, 1232 Labrosse St. (1851)
- St. Paul's Episcopal Church (Church of the Messiah), 231 E. Grand Blvd. and E. Lafayette St. (originally northeast corner of Congress and Shelby) (1852)
- Traugott Schmidt Company, east of 510 Monroe St. (1853)
- John Mason house, 1705 Sixth St. (1853)
- Fort Street Presbyterian Church, 631 W. Fort (1855)
- Most Holy Trinity Roman Catholic Church, 1062 Porter St. (1856)
- Braddock/Crane house, 1334 Labrosse St. (1855-65)
- Saint John's Episcopal Church, 2326 Woodward Ave. (1861)
- Christ Church, 960 E. Jefferson Ave. (1863)
- Joseph H. Esterling house, 2245 Wabash (1864)

Detroit Central Market (also known as City Hall Market, the Vegetable Shed, or "Mich. Grand Ave. Market" in an 1873 map) operated from 1861 to near the end of the century, located at what is now Cadillac Square Park. It has been reconstructed at The Henry Ford in Dearborn.

The post hospital of Fort Gratiot, dating from the 1820s, remains standing thanks to reconstruction by the Port Huron Museums. The original site of the fort was south of the Blue Water Bridge in Port Huron. The renovated structure is located in Lighthouse Park in the 2800 block of Conger Street, Port Huron.

Appendix

I. Chronology of Major Life Events

1822, Oct. 11 – born
1836, Aug. – family moved to Detroit
1840, Jan./Feb. – Charles Stuart Tripler arrived in Detroit
1841, Mar. 2 – married
1842, May 8 – first child (Charles Stuart) born
1843, Sept. 7 – child #1 dies
1843, Dec. 19 – second child (Alice Hunt) born
1846, Feb. 19 – third child (Charles Stuart) born
1846, summer – husband departed for service in Mexico
1849, Sept. 8 – fourth child (Ellen Mackintosh) born
1850 – moved to Fort Gratiot
1850, Oct. 8 – child #4 dies
1851, Aug. 21 – fifth child (Ellen Cass) born
1856 – reunion with husband after four years apart
1856 – moved to Kentucky
1856, Nov. 13 – sixth child (Edgar Mackin) born
1858, July 4 – child #6 dies
1859, Mar. 17 – seventh child (Edward Townsend) born
1860, Dec. 21 – eighth child (Eunice Montgomery Meigs) born
1861, Apr. – moved back to Detroit; husband ordered East
1861, Aug. 12 – husband became Medical Director, Army of the Potomac
1861, Dec. – joined her husband in Washington

1862, Mar. 25 – returned to Detroit; husband accompanied Army to James Peninsula
1862, Jul. 4 – husband relieved of duties with Army of the Potomac, returned to Detroit
1862, Dec. 25 – ninth child (Henry Hunt) born
1866, Oct. 20 – husband dies
1871, Feb. 15 – child #2 dies
1900 – moved to Nebraska
1906, Jan. 13 – child #3 dies
1910, Mar. 28 – dies
1910, Mar. 31 – interment in Historic Elmwood Cemetery

II. Announcement of Death of Dr. Tripler

Adjutant General's Office,
Washington, October 27, 1866.
General Orders, No. 89.
The following notice of the decease of a distinguished officer of the Medical Department of the army, by the chief of his Department, is published to the army:
Surgeon General's Office,
Washington, October 23, 1866.
To the Adjutant General, U. S. Army:

Sir: I have the honor to report the death, at Cincinnati, on the 20th instant, of Brevet Brigadier General C.S. Tripler, Surgeon, U.S. Army, Medical Director, Department of the Lakes.

Entering the army as assistant surgeon, October, 1830, General Tripler served continuously for thirty-six years, during which time he held with credit to himself and advantage to the government, positions of high trust and responsibility, taking part in the Seminole war, the war with Mexico, the occupation of California, and being the first Medical Director of the Army of the Potomac.

His skilful [sic] administration and conscientious discharge of duty, has been rewarded by three brevets for 'faithful and meritorious services.' The Medical Corps possesses in his distinguished career a bright example of the union of great professional attainments, with the military zeal and pride of an officer, and those qualities which mark the christian gentleman.

Very respectfully, your obedient servant,
J.K. Barnes,
Surgeon General.
By Order of the Secretary Of War:
E. D. Townsend,
Assistant Adjutant General.[234]

III. Legislative History of Royalty Bill

According to EHT's memoir, she sought financial recognition for the Government's use of Dr. Tripler's *Manual* a year or so after she started receiving a pension as his widow. Nothing came of her attempt. In 1876, the Senate Committee on Pensions issued an unfavorable report concerning any additional relief.

EHT relayed that Congressman Lord of Michigan introduced a bill to compensate her for the Government's use of the work. Lord served between 1881 and 1883; the *Journal* of the House of Representatives records that he introduced a petition for relief on her behalf on May 22, 1882.[235] This step came in the 1st Session of the 47th Congress.

Formal legislation appears to have been first introduced in the 48th Congress, in the U.S. Senate, in the form of S. 782. After passing the Senate, and referral, the House Committee on Military Affairs reported it adversely, and it was postponed indefinitely on February 19, 1884.

Two bills were introduced in the 50th Congress, 1st Session,

---

234. *The Medical and Surgical Reporter*, Vol. XV (Nov. 10, 1866), 408.
235. *Journal of the House of Representatives of the United States, Being the First Session of the Forty-Seventh Congress* (Washington: Government Printing Office, 1881), 1303.

both in the Senate (S. 946) and the House (H.R. 2513). No action was taken beyond the reporting back of the House bill from the Committee on Military Affairs.

In the 51st Congress, 1st Session, a bill (S. 562) passed the Senate and was referred to committee in the House. There, it died.

In the 52nd Congress, 1st Session, a bill (S. 293) passed the Senate and was referred to committee in the House, where it died.

In the 53rd Congress, 2nd Session, a bill (S. 910) passed the Senate and was referred in the House. The Committee on Claims reported the bill adversely with the recommendation that it not pass; it did not.

In the 54th Congress, 1st Session, a bill (S. 314) passed the Senate; after referral, the House Committee on Claims reported it out with a recommendation that it pass. It did not.

In the 55th Congress, a bill (S. 1101) passed the Senate and was referred to House committee.

In the 56th Congress, 1st Session, a bill (S. 147) passed the Senate and again received a favorable recommendation from a House committee (on Claims).

In the 57th Congress, 1st Session, a bill (S. 2055) received a favorable recommendation from the Senate Committee on Military Affairs.

In the 58th Congress, a bill (S. 3820) received a favorable recommendation from the Senate Committee on Military Affairs. After passing the Senate, it received action in the House Committee on Claims via amendment.

In the 59th Congress, a bill (S. 3820) was enacted, effective January 25, 1907, specifying:[236]

---

236. *The Statutes at Large of the United States of America from December, 1905, to March, 1907*, Vol. XXXIV, Part 2 (Washington: Government Printing Office, 1907), 2308. The bill was introduced by Senator Burkett on January 29, 1906, and referred to committee (*Congressional Record*, 59th Congress, First Session, Vol. XL (Washington: Government Printing Office, 1906), 1670). It was reported out of the Committee on Claims with amendment on April 3, 1906 (S. Rept. No. 2305) (id. 4631) and passed the Senate on April 11 with approval of the amendment to reduce payment from $10,000 to $3,000 (id. 5037). It

That there be paid to Eunice Tripler, widow of Surgeon Charles S. Tripler, United States Army, out of any money in the Treasury not otherwise appropriated, the sum of three thousand dollars, for services by the said Charles S. Tripler in his lifetime in preparing, superintending, and directing the publication of a manual for the use of medical officers of the Army of the United States: *Provided*, That payment of the above sum shall be a bar to any further claim against the Government for the use of the book herein referred to.

IV. Other Civil War Hunts
A.

The relation closest to Eunice Hunt Tripler was son Charles Stuart Tripler, named for his father, and the second child from the marriage to hold that name (the first died at 18 months). He was born on February 19, 1846, in Detroit.

He entered the service of the United States Army on June 18, 1863, commissioned 2nd Lieutenant as of June 18. Enrolled and appointed, Company E, 96th New York Volunteer Infantry Regiment. Promoted to 1st Lieutenant, November 25, 1863, to date from August 17, 1863. Mustered in Company A, on December 9, 1863.

The date of his birth is written in the family Bible. The record of his service comes from official records. He was 17 years old when commissioned – and, therefore, likely misrepresented his age in order to serve.

The 96th New York Infantry was organized at Plattsburgh, New York, in early 1862 and mustered in for three-years' service on February 20, 1862. It was initially assigned to the IV Corps of the Army of the Potomac.

---

passed the House without debate on January 19, 1907 (*Congressional Record*, 59th Congress, Second Session, Vol. XLI (Washington: Government Printing Office, 1907), 1389-1390), was enrolled and signed on January 22 and 23 (id. 1534, 1538), and signed by President Theodore Roosevelt on the 25th (id., Jan. 29, 1907), 1866.

When Tripler joined the regiment, it was assigned to the District of the Albemarle, Department of North Carolina. It participated in expeditions in North Carolina in the latter half of 1863. For the Overland Campaign in Spring 1864, it transferred to the XVIII Corps, Army of the James, and participated in the following actions:

- operations on the south side of the James River and against Petersburg and Richmond, May 4–28
- occupation of Bermuda Hundred and City Point, Va., May 5
- operations against Fort Darling, May 12–16
- Battle of Drury's Bluff, May 14–16
- Bermuda Hundred, May 16–27
- Battles about Cold Harbor, June 1–12
- as part of the XXIV Corps, siege operations against Petersburg and Richmond, June 16, 1864 to April 2, 1865, including Battles of Chaffin's Farm, New Market Heights, September 28–30, Battle of Fair Oaks, October 27–28, 1864
- occupation of Richmond, April 3, 1865[237]

C.S. Tripler was discharged from the volunteer service on August 31, 1865.

On February 20, 1866, the Senate confirmed his appointment to 1st Lieutenant in the Twelfth Infantry Regiment, effective November 24, 1865. He received a promotion to Captain effective January 22, 1867. He served until resignation effective September 1, 1873.

In 1873, he married Emilie Augusta Abell (1847–1920). They had two children together, but it appears that Tripler left the marriage. He married Emma Schulz in 1897; she was born in 1876 and died in 1944. He died January 13, 1906, and was buried in the old city cemetery of Tacoma, Washington, as was his second wife.

Eunice mentioned her son in a letter to granddaughter Emilie

---

237. Frederick H. Dyer, *A Compendium of the War of the Rebellion* (Des Moines: Dyer Publishing Co., 1908), 194.

Alice Harriette Tripler Bertsch, the daughter of Emilie Augusta Abell, during the early 1890s, lamenting that no one knew where he was, whether dead or alive even – "but do keep praying for him."

The 1880 census shows Emilie Augusta Abell Tripler living with her father and listed as widow.

In 1885, former Captain Tripler wrote an article to the editor for a San Francisco newspaper, entitled "Jefferson Davis in Prison":

★ ★ ★

You have asked me for some short account of the "prison life of Jefferson Davis," as remembered by me. I gladly comply with your request, both to oblige a friend and to correct erroneous impressions which seem to exist. I was in 1865 First Lieutenant in the Twelfth U.S. Infantry, and in the absence of my Captain commanded E Company of the First Battalion of that regiment. Early in October I was ordered to Fort Monroe, and reported for duty to General N.A. Miles, Major-General U.S. Volunteers, now Brigadier-General, U.S.A., who was in command.[238] The Fifth Artillery, U.S.A., General Burton[239] commanding, was then stationed there. My rank as Lieutenant subjected me to detail as officer of the guard, and as such I had for the twenty-four hours of my detail immediate charge of our distinguished prisoner, my orders being "not to allow him out of my sight during my tour of duty." Mr. Davis was confined to a room in Carroll Hall, which was designed as quarters for Lieutenants, who are entitled to two rooms only, so all the rooms, except the mess hall and library are in suites of two rooms each.[240]

---

238. Nelson A. Miles (1839-1925), Brigadier-General of volunteers as of May 12, 1864, Major-General of volunteers as of October 21, 1865, at the age of 26.
239. Henry S. Burton (1819-1869), graduate of West Point in the Class of 1839.
240. Davis was originally housed in a casemate from May-October 1865, when he was removed to the former officers' quarters until released in May 1867. *The War of the Rebellion*, Series II (Washington: Government Printing Office, 1899), Volume VIII, 755-760.

[Tripler provided a diagram, which was printed in the paper at this point] …

As was the custom, on my first tour of duty as Officer of the Guard, I was introduced by my predecessor to Mr. Davis, thus: "Mr. Davis, Mr. Tripler of the Twelfth." Mr. Davis said: "Are you Stuart Tripler?" I said: "yes sir." He then said he remembered my grandmother (Mrs. Hunt) and had very pleasant recollections of my father (Surgeon Tripler of the Army). We had that first day no further conversation until the time came for his daily walk around the parapet. At that time the officer of the day came, accompanied by two negro prisoners, unlocked the door, when Mr. Davis, dressed in snuff-colored clothes, with a "Raglan" overcoat and soft, high-crowned, black felt hat, stepped into my room.

General Miles entered at this time with the daily papers which were on a table in Mr. D's room. The prisoners commenced at once to clean up the room and we left by way of the gallery crossing a little bridge to the parapet, … in the following order: Mr. Davis and officers of the guard, ten paces behind two sentries, a couple of paces behind them the Officer of the Day, and lastly, some distance off, General Miles strolled along, reading. We took our time, and Mr. Davis by his instructive and most entertaining conversation rendered this a most delightful duty.

He seemed to know everything. He had the unusual faculty of drawing a young man out and making him show his best side. We would sometimes stop abreast of the water battery, in front of the commanding officers' quarters, and recline on the crest of the works, where he would relate pleasant stories of the old army, ask after common friends, and often give me "points" in my profession which were invaluable.

… On our return Dr. Cooper's servant came in with Mr. Davis' lunch. All his meals were supplied from Dr. Cooper's[241] table and Mrs. Cooper was a notable housewife, and the markets of Fortress Monroe

---

241. Surgeon George E. Cooper.

were well supplied; you may be sure Mr. Davis did not suffer. The only request he ever made me during the time I was stationed there, was to bring him a few apples each time I came on guard, which I did. I rather think he asked me for the sake of letting me think I was doing him a favor in return for his exceeding kindness to my grandmother when he was Secretary of War. He could make a request in such a way that you felt he had conferred a favor on you in preferring it. C.C. Clay was confined in the rooms directly beneath Mr. Davis, but had Mrs. Clay with him, and was not guarded as Mr. Davis was.[242]

Mrs. Clay used to send sometimes a pitcher of punch to Mr. Davis. My orders not forbidding it, the pitcher was always passed in. Mr. Davis was supplied with good cigars by his friends. I know they were good, because Mr. Davis remarked that "smokers are gregarious, and I can't enjoy a cigar alone," and offered me one nearly every night, after he had assumed his most santanic-looking [sic] night robes – he wore a red-flannel nightgown, cap and drawers. He was never annoyed, insulted or worried during his stay. Gen. Miles was coldly civil and others "officially polite." I perhaps, and as was natural, was more kindly disposed, but I never exceeded the letter of my instructions. I think Mr. Davis will himself give the lie to the exaggerated accounts of his sufferings. Imprisonment is not pleasant under the most favorable circumstances, and no fallen chief of a great movement could have expected or received more considerate treatment than did Mr. Davis.

Yours truly,
Chas. S. Tripler,
Late Capt. Twelfth Infantry, U.S.A.[243]

★ ★ ★

---

242. Clement C. Clay (1816-1882), Confederate States Senator.
243. *Daily Alta California*, July 27, 1885, Vol. 39, No. 12918, 8. Corroboration of this first meeting of Tripler and Davis appears in John J. Craven, *Prison Life of Jefferson Davis* (London: Sampson Low, Son, and Marston, 1866), 119-120, except for the date, which was June 24, 1865.

He was convicted in Oregon of forgery, and his first wife, Emilie Augusta Abell Tripler, divorced him on grounds of desertion. An associate tried to obtain leniency on the forgery charge based partly on the fact that the late Captain was badly wounded at the Battle of the Wilderness in May 1864.

Charles S. and Emma S. are buried beneath a common gravestone with "Tripler" as the superscription. Her portion states the years of birth and death. His says, "Capt. U.S.A."

B.

Henry Jackson Hunt (1819-1889), named after forebears, was the son of Samuel Wellington Hunt. His father attended but did not graduate from West Point and died in 1829. The son graduated in the middle of the Class of 1839 and went on to a momentous career.

C.

Lewis Cass Hunt (1824-1886) was born in Wisconsin, another son of Samuel Wellington Hunt. He graduated 33rd of 38 in the West Point Class of 1847, along with Ambrose Burnside, Charles Griffin, Henry Heth, A.P. Hill, and Orlando B. Willcox. As Colonel of the 92nd New York Infantry Regiment, he was wounded at the Battle of Seven Pines. He served in the U.S. Army until his death.

D.

George Wellington Hunt (1833-1881) was Captain of Company C of the 5th Michigan Cavalry Regiment. Commissioned on August 14, 1862, age 29, he served until resigning effective March 23, 1863. The Michigan Cavalry Brigade, consisting of the 1st, 5th, 6th, and 7th regiments, was formed on December 12, 1862. His father was William Brown Hunt, brother to Thomas.

Postscript:

The Female Union Doctor

Eunice Hunt Tripler's story is framed by the societal limitations that existed in the 19th century when women did not enjoy the opportunities that later generations would. Still, Tripler's efforts to aid her soldier husband in his work at the office, to lobby on his behalf within the Army, the Congress, and the Lincoln Administration, and to seek her due in government recognition and royalties for a book Dr. Tripler wrote during their marriage, all show the fiber of a female who did not constrain herself within traditional models of feminine behavior, as did her outspokenness on behalf of the Union while posted in a slave State. That she undertook such conduct while a wife, mother to nine children, and widow for nearly a half-century speaks volumes.

Some women of the era did break through the bounds of convention. Ironically, one individual did so in Dr. Tripler's profession and in a military capacity. Although born and raised in New York, and with no evidence she ever visited this State, there is a Michigan connection.

On a wall inside a United States Army facility in western lower Michigan is a plaque explaining its naming as the "Walker Army Reserve Center." Located at 3870 3 Mile Road NW, with a postal address of Grand Rapids and zip code of 49534, the building's main sign indicates its actual location within the City of Walker, Michigan. The municipality's name dates to an act of the Michigan Legislature approved on December 30, 1837 – but that is not the full reason for the Center's identity.[244]

The Walker Army Reserve Center is named for a Civil War era Medal of Honor recipient – Dr. Mary Edwards Walker. Extensive research and sponsorship of the nomination package by a local Michigander, himself a retired Army officer, resulted in naming this medical group headquarters after someone whose military service was worthy of the honor. The plaque reads:

During the American Civil War she was commissioned as an assistant surgeon in the Union army, becoming the first woman to hold such a commission. She worked as a field surgeon near the front lines. She was a prisoner of war in Richmond, VA. for four months. In 1865, she was awarded the Congressional Medal of Honor for services performed on the field of battle. Subsequently, she practiced medicine in Washington, D.C.

According to the *New York Times*, "The medal was awarded to her by President Andrew Johnson on Nov. 11, 1865. Generals William T. Sherman and George H. Thomas had recommended the medal; President Lincoln had signed their testimonial before his death."[245] According to the historical society of Oswego, New York, the inscription on the medal reads: "The Congress. To Dr. Mary E. Walker. A.A. Surgeon, U.S.A. Nov. 11th 1865". According to the Congressional Medal of Honor Society,[246] the "details" are: Rank: Contract Surgeon; Conflict/Era: U.S. Civil War; Military Service Branch: U.S. Army; Medal Of Honor Action Date: 1861 – 1864; Medal Of Honor Action Place: North Carolina, D.C., Tennessee, Georgia, USA". The Society also gives the text of the "Citation" as:

---

244. *Acts of the Legislature of the State of Michigan; Passed at the Adjourned Session of 1837, and the Regular Session of 1838* (Detroit: John S. Bagg, 1838), 15. Why the choice of "Walker", according to various sources, remains a mystery.
245. "The Case of Dr. Walker, Only Woman To Win (and Lose) the Medal of Honor," June 4, 1977, p. 38.
246. https://www.cmohs.org/recipients/mary-e-walker

★ ★ ★

Whereas it appears from official reports that Dr. Mary E. Walker, a graduate of medicine, "has rendered valuable service to the Government, and her efforts have been earnest and untiring in a variety of ways," and that she was assigned to duty and served as an assistant surgeon in charge of female prisoners at Louisville, Ky., upon the recommendation of Maj. Gens. Sherman and Thomas, and faithfully served as contract surgeon in the service of the United States, and has devoted herself with much patriotic zeal to the sick and wounded soldiers, both in the field and hospitals, to the detriment of her own health, and has also endured hardships as a prisoner of war four months in a Southern prison while acting as contract surgeon; and

Whereas by reason of her not being a commissioned officer in the military service, a brevet or honorary rank cannot, under existing laws, be conferred upon her; and

Whereas in the opinion of the President an honorable recognition of her services and sufferings should be made;

It is ordered, That a testimonial thereof shall be hereby made and given to the said Dr. Mary E. Walker, and that the usual medal of honor for meritorious services be given her.

Given under my hand in the city of Washington, D.C., this 11th day of November, A.D. 1865.

Andrew Johnson

Born on November 26, 1832, she died February 21, 1919, at the age of 86.

On May 25, 2022, a congressional entity known as the Naming Commission, created by the 2021 National Defense Authorization Act, issued an initial recommendation that Fort A.P. Hill near Bowling Green, Virginia, be renamed for Dr. Walker. The Commission's final report is due to Congress in October 2022.

★ ★ ★

Bibliography

Acts of the Legislature of the State of Michigan; Passed at the Adjourned Session of 1837, and the Regular Session of 1838 (Detroit: John S. Bagg, 1838)

Barnett, Le Roy & Rosentreter, Roger. *Michigan's Early Military Forces* (Detroit: Wayne State University Press, 2003)

Chernow, Ron. *Grant* (New York: Penguin Press, 2017)

Congressional Globe, 36th Congress, 1st Session

Congressional Globe, 37th Congress, 2nd Session

Congressional Record

Cooper, Edward S. *Traitors: The Secession Period, November 1860-July 1861* (Madison: Fairleigh Dickinson University Press, 2008)

Craven, John J. *Prison Life of Jefferson Davis* (London: Sampson Low, Son, and Marston, 1866)

Daily Alta California

Detroit Daily Free Press

Detroit Free Press

Detroit Medical News

Dickey, J.D. *Empire of Mud: The Secret History of Washington, DC* (Guilford: Lyons Press, 2014)

Dyer, Frederick H. *A Compendium of the War of the Rebellion* (Des Moines: Dyer Publishing Co., 1908)

Edwards, Albert. *Panama: The Canal, the Country, and the People* (New York: Macmillan Co., 1912)

Eicher, John H. & Eicher, David J. *Civil War High Commands* (Stanford: Stanford University Press, 2001)

Farmer, Silas. *The History of Detroit and Michigan or The Metropolis Illustrated* (Detroit: Silas Farmer & Co., 1889)

Green, Constance M. *The Secret City: A History of Race Relations in the Nation's Capital* (Princeton: Princeton University Press, 1967)

Hamilton, John C. ed. *The Works of Alexander Hamilton; Comprising His Correspondence, and His Political and Official Writings*, Vol. I (New York: John F. Trow, 1851)

Hershock, Martin J. *The Paradox of Progress: Economic Change, Individual Enterprise, and Political Culture in Michigan, 1837-1878* (Athens: Ohio University Press, 2003)

Journal of the House of Representatives of the United States

Kelton, Dwight H. *Annals of Fort Mackinac* (Detroit: Detroit Free Press Printing Co., 1887)

Lanman, Charles. *The Red Book of Michigan; A Civil, Military and Biographical History* (Detroit: E.B. Smith & Co., 1871)

Leake, Paul. *History of Detroit*, Vol. I (Chicago: Lewis Pub. Co., 1912)

Lee, Sidney ed. *Dictionary of National Biography*, Vol. LVIII (New York: Macmillan Co., 1899)

Levasseur, Auguste. *Lafayette in America, in 1824 and 1825* (Philadelphia: Carey & Lea, 1829), Vols. I & II

Longacre, Edward G. *The Man Behind the Guns: A Military Biography of General Henry J. Hunt, Commander Of Artillery, Army Of The Potomac* (Cambridge: Da Capo Press, 2003)

Marryat, Frederick. *A Diary in America, with Remarks on Its Institutions* (Paris: A. & W. Galignani & Co., 1839)

McClellan, George B. *McClellan's Own Story: The War for the Union, the Soldiers Who Fought It, the Civilians Who Directed It and His Relations to It and to Them* (New York: Charles L. Webster & Co., 1887)

The Medical and Surgical Reporter, Vol. XV (Nov. 10, 1866)

Minneapolis Star

Morris, Maud Burr. *An Old Washington Mansion* (reprint from *Records of the Columbia Historical Society, Washington, D.C.*, vol. 21, 1918)

New York Times

Palmer, Friend. *Early Days in Detroit* (Detroit: Hunt & June, 1906)

The Personal Memoirs of Julia Dent Grant, John Y. Simon ed. (New York: G.P. Putnam's Sons, 1975)

Quist, John W. ed. *Michigan's War: The Civil War in Documents* (Athens: Ohio University Press, 2019)

Robertson, John. *Michigan in the War* (Lansing: W.S. George & Co., 1882)

Ross, Ishbel. *The General's Wife: The Life of Mrs. Ulysses S. Grant* (New York: Dodd, Mead & Co., 1959)

Sanger, George P. ed. *The Statutes at Large*, Vol. XII (Boston: Little, Brown & Co., 1863)

Sears, Stephen W. *George B. McClellan: The Young Napoleon* (New York: Da Capo Press, 1999)

Senate Committee Report No. 96, 36th Congress, 1st Session

Senate Executive Journal

Simon, John Y. ed. *Papers of Ulysses S. Grant*, Vol. II (Carbondale: Southern Illinois University Press, 1967)

Smith, Hal H. "Historic Washington Homes" in *Records of the Columbia Historical Society, Washington, D.C.*, Vol. 11 (1908)

Smith, Margaret Bayard. *The First Forty Years of Washington Society*, Gaillard Hunt ed. (New York: Charles Scribner's Sons, 1906)

Statistical Report on the Sickness and Mortality in the Army of the United States, Compiled from the Records of the Surgeon General's Office, Embracing a Period of Sixteen Years, from January, 1839, to January 1855, Senate Exec. Doc. No. 96, 34th Congress, 1st Session (Washington: A.O.P. Nicholson, 1856)

The Statutes at Large of the United States of America from December, 1905, to March, 1907, Vol. XXXIV, Part 2 (Washington: Government Printing Office, 1907)

Symonds, Craig L. *Joseph E. Johnston: A Civil War Biography* (New York: W.W. Norton & Co., 1994)

Tripler, Charles S. *The Causes, Nature, and Treatment of Scurvy: A Paper Read Before the Covington and Newport (Ky.) Medical Society* (n.p., ca. 1858)

Tripler, Charles S. *The Duties of Physicians in Relation to Popular Medical Delusions: An Address Delivered Before the Covington and*

Newport Medical Society, June 14, 1859 (Covington: S.G. Cobb, 1859)

Tripler, Charles S. *Manual of the Medical Officer of the Army of the United States, Part I, Recruiting and the Inspection of Recruits, by Charles S. Tripler, M.D., Surgeon U.S.A.; Fellow of the College of Physicians and Surgeons of the University of the State of New York* (Cincinnati: Wrightson & Co., 1858)

Tripler, Charles S. *Remarks on Delirium Tremens, or the Irritative Fever of Drunkenness: An Inaugural Dissertation, Submitted to the Examination of the Faculty of the College of Physicians and Surgeons of the University of the State of New York* (New York: J. Seymour, [April 3,] 1827)

Tripler, Charles S. & Blackman, George Curtis. *Hand-Book for Military Surgeons* (Cincinnati: Robert Clarke & Co., 1861)

Tripler, Eunice. *Some Notes of her Personal Recollections* (New York: The Grafton Press, 1910)

U.S. Census

The War of the Rebellion: A Compilation of the Official Records of the Union and Confederate Armies, Series I (Washington: Government Printing Office, 1881, 1884), Volume V, Volume XI, part I; Series II, Volume VIII (1899)

Wellings, James H. Directory of the City of Detroit; and Register of Michigan, for the Year 1846 (Detroit: A.S. Williams, 1846)

Willard, Emma. *History of the United States, or, Republic of America* (New York: A.S. Barnes & Co., 1845)

Wood, Edwin O. *Historic Mackinac: The Historical, Picturesque and Legendary Features of the Mackinac Country* (New York: Macmillan Co., 1918)

Wright, Richard J. ed. *The John Hunt Memoirs: Early Years of the Maumee Basin, 1812-1835* (Maumee: Maumee Valley Historical Society, n.d.)

Index

A
Abell, Emilie Augusta, 104–105, 108
Adams, John Quincy, 15, 87
Adams, Mount, 55
Addison, Joseph, 93n
African Americans ("negro"), 27, 106
alcoholic beverages, 52n
Amherstburg, 2, 5, 75
Anderson, Robert, 34, 78
Armitage, William E., 82
Army of the Potomac, xiv, 15n, 35n, 62, 64, 65n, 66, 71, 72, 72n, 76n, 79, 94, 99, 100, 103
Arthur, Louis A., xvi, 64n
Aztec Club/Society, 1n, 35

B
Bache, Matilda Wilkins, 67, 68n
Baldwin, Henry P., 87
Baltimore & Ohio Railroad, 20n
"Baptism of Pocahontas," 14
Barnes, Joseph K., 75, 80, 84, 101
Battle of Brownstown, xv, 4
Battle of Lundy's Lane, 27
Battle of Yorktown, xv
Bell, Frances Fanny, 20
Bell, John, 20
Bellows, Henry W., 69
Bernard, Simon, 9–10
Bernard, Sophie, 10
Biddle House Hotel, 28, 77n, 97
Bissell, Charles, 63, 72, 80
Bissell, William Henry Augustus, 22
Blackman, George Curtis, 55n, 81
Blair, Montgomery, 12

Bonneville, Benjamin L.E., 42n
Brady, Hugh, 27, 38
Brady, Mathew, xv
Brooks, Preston, 23n
Brown, Harvey, 25
Brown, Jacob, 12, 88
Brown, Stephen, 29
Buchanan, James, 14, 57n
Buchanan, Robert C., 35
Buckner, Simon Bolivar, 38
Burkett, Elmer J., 84, 102n
Burlingame, Anson, 22
Burnside, Ambrose E., 72, 108
Burton, Henry S., 105

C
California, xiii, 10, 39, 40, 42, 52–54, 61, 72, 82, 86n, 89, 97, 100, 107n
Canfield, Augustus, 39, 53
Capitol of Michigan, 22
Casey, Silas, 35
Cass, Elizabeth Spencer, 7n, 15, 16n, 19, 53
Cass, Lewis, 5, 7, 12n, 15, 19, 21, 39n, 53
Cass, Mary Sophia, 39n
Cass, Matilda Frances, 7n, 12
Chandler, Zachariah, 57n, 71–72, 73–74
Chaplin, Abby S., 4n
Chapman, John Gadsby, 14
Childs, Thomas, 31, 32n
Cincinnati Medical College, 55, 61
Cincinnati Observatory, 55n

Clay, Clement Claiborne, 57, 107
Clay, Henry, 11
Clitz, John, 24
Clitz, Mary, 24
College of Physicians and Surgeons, 30n, 83n, 85n, 89, 92n
Columbia College, New York, 30, 89, 90
Columbus, Oh., 79, 81, 90
Connor, Catherine Elizabeth, 27n
Cooper, George E., 106
Cooper, James Fenimore, 52–53, 55
Crimean War, 61
Crittenden, John J., 56–57, 60

D

Davis, Jefferson Finis, 51, 56–59, 105–107
Department of the Lakes, 73, 79, 89, 100
Detroit Club, 28n
Detroit, Mich., xiii–xvii, 2–6, 12n, 13, 15, 19, 21–24, 26–28, 31–32, 37–40, 42, 52, 54, 55n, 73, 75, 76n, 77, 79–82, 86n, 87–89, 90n, 92n, 93, 94, 97–98, 99–100, 103
Dickinson, Sally, 20n
Drum, Richard C., 84

E

Eaton, John H., 30
Edmunds, George F., 83
Election Day, 28
Emory, William H., 67, 68n
Euclid, 23

F

Farnsworth, James Harvey, 27
Farquhar, Francis U., 82
Farrand, David Osborn, 74
Forsyth, Alice M.S. (or Forsythe), xv–xvi, 3
Forsyth, Maria, 22n

Forsyth, Robert Allen (or Forsythe), xvi, 2–3
Forsythe, Robert, 5, 19, 22–23, 26–27
Fort Detroit, 4n
Fort Gratiot, 39–40, 54, 89, 98, 99
"Fort Street Girls," 22n
Fort Wayne, Detroit, 22, 81
Fort Yuma, 88

G

gambling, 18, 34
Gardiner, John W.T., 35
Gibson, George, 9, 58
Goldsborough, Charles W., 8
Grand Island, Neb., xvi, 94
Grant, Frederick Dent, 38n
Grant, Julia Dent, xiii, 37, 38n, 77–78, 88, 97
Grant, Ulysses S., xiii, xv, 37–38, 39, 42, 52, 69, 72–73, 77, 80, 88, 97
Gratiot, Charles Chouteau, 11, 14
Griffin, Levi T., 84
Gwin, William M., 53

H

Hale, Edward Everett, xv
Halleck, Henry W., 88
Hamilton, Alexander, 1
Hamilton, Schuyler, 63
Hammond, William A., 80
Hand, George E., 23
Harney, William S., 31
Harper Hospital, 79n
Harrison, William Henry, 27
Harrison's Landing, Va., 73
Hawley, William, 7–8
Hayes, Rutherford B., xv, 87
Heintzelman, Margaret Stuart (or Heintzleman), 67, 69, 70
Heintzelman, Samuel P. (or Heintzleman), 67n, 69, 71
Historic Elmwood Cemetery, xv, xvii, 81, 82, 93–94, 100
Hooker, Joseph, xiii, 52, 72, 81

Houston, Samuel, 43
Howard, Jacob M., 73–74
Hull, William, 4
Hunt, George Wellington, 108
Hunt, Henry Jackson (b. 1786), 3n
Hunt, Henry Jackson (b. 1819), xvi, 4, 25, 64, 67, 72, 78–79, 81, 83, 108
Hunt, Lewis Cass, 38, 108
Hunt, Samuel Wellington, xvi, 108
Hunt, Thomas, xv, 3, 4n, 16, 58n, 94
Hunt, Thomas V., xv, 1, 2, 3
Hunt, William Brown, 108

I
Irving, Washington, 11
Isthmus of Panama, 40–41, 52

J
Jackson, Andrew, 8, 11, 15, 20, 21, 89
Jefferson, Joseph Jr., 18
Jefferson, Joseph III, 18n
Jesup, Thomas S. (or Jessup), 58
"Jim," 33
Johnson, Andrew, 80, 90, 110, 111
Johnston, Joseph E., xiii, 11, 25, 39

K
Kane, Elisha Kent, 41
Kemble, Charles, 18n
Kemble, Frances Anne, 17, 18n
Kercheval, Benjamin B., 22n
Kercheval, Maria, 2, 5, 22n
Kinzie, John, 19

L
Lafayette, Marquis de, 9–10, 94
Lake Superior, 25
Latrobe, Benjamin H., 8n
Ledyard, Henry, 12n
Lee, Robert E., xiii, 23n, 35, 73, 79
Leghorn hat, 5
Letterman, Jonathan, xviii
Lincoln, Abraham, xiv, 12, 18, 23n, 63, 64, 66, 68, 71, 73, 90, 94, 109, 110

Lincoln, Mary Todd, xiv, 64, 67, 68–69, 71, 94
Lincoln, Robert, 68
Lord, Henry W., 83, 101
Lytle, Margaret, xvi

M
Mackinac Island, 24, 32, 53
Maclin, Sackfield, 60n
Macomb, Alexander (or McComb, Mc-Comb), 7, 12, 88, 94
Macomb, Jane (or McComb), 12
Marcy, Mary Ellen, 67n
Marryat, Frederick, 21, 22n
Maury, Dabney H., xv
McClellan, George B., xiv, xviii, 56, 62, 65n, 66–67, 71, 72, 73, 83, 88, 90, 94
McCoskry, Samuel A., 22, 24, 26, 80
McDowell, Irwin, 71, 72, 78
McLane, Louis, 11n
McLane, Lydia Mulligan Sims, 11n
McMillan, James, 84
Meade, George G., 72, 79
Meigs, Montgomery C., 64
Mexican-American War, xiii, xiv, 1n, 16n, 28, 32, 34, 35n, 36, 42n, 73, 94
Miles, Nelson A., 105, 106, 107
Military Order of the Loyal Legion of the United States, 1n, 87
Mitchel, Ormsby M. (or Mitchell), 55
Monroe, James, 87
Montreal, Que., 4
Moore, John, 84

N
Nellie, 6
Newport Barracks, Ky., 32, 54–56, 58–61, 64, 67n, 69, 81, 83, 89, 92
Norris, George W., 85
Norvell, John, 26, 27

O
"Octagon House," 10n

Olmsted, Frederick Law, xv
Ord, Edward Otho Cresap, 9, 83

P
Palmer, Thomas W., 84
Patterson, Robert, 63
Pemberton, John C., 38–39
Peninsula Campaign, xv, xviii, 38n, 62, 67n, 72, 73, 82n
Pennsylvania Avenue, 9n, 10, 16, 17, 21, 65
Pitcher, Zina, 58n, 81
Pleasanton, Alfred, 15n
Pleasanton, Augustus James, 15n
Pleasanton, Clementina, 14, 15n
Pleasanton, Laura, 15n
Pleasanton, Stephen, 15n
Pope, John, xv, 72
Porter, Andrew, 64
Porter, Fitz John, xv, 35, 36

R
Rains, Gabriel James, 40n
Ramsey, Alexander, 14, 15n
Rawlins, John A., 80
religious practice, 35
"Rhoderick," 11
Riley, Bennett C., 32n
Rosecrans, William S., 83, 90
Royalty Bill, 101

S
Satterlee, Richard S., 82
Sault Ste. Marie, Mich., 24-25
Schulz, Emma, 104
Scott, Walter, 5, 6n, 55
Scott, Winfield, xiii, xvii, 12, 24-25, 27, 32, 33, 34, 35, 36, 61-62, 63, 88
Seminole conflicts, 9n, 31, 94, 100
"Seven Buildings," 17, 65
Seward, William H., 57, 64, 68-69
sewing, 19, 74
Shenandoah Valley, 63
Sheridan, Irene Rucker, 88

Sheridan, Philip H., 88, 94
Sherman, John, 74, 83
Sherman, William T., xiii, 52, 61, 83, 88, 110, 111
Sherman, William T. Jr., 61n
slavery, xiii, xvii, 6, 7, 71n
smallpox (or small-pox), 7, 8n, 30, 65, 70
Smith, William Farrar, 66
Snelling, Josiah, 4
social customs, 13
Society of the Cincinnati, 1, 35n
St. John's Episcopal Church, Washington, 7, 8, 10n, 16, 65
St. Paul's Episcopal Church, Detroit, 22, 24, 26, 98
Stewart, Duncan, 34, 36
Stone, Charles P., 52
Stoneman, George, xv
Sumner, Charles, xi, 23n
Sykes, George, xv

T
Taney, Roger B., 12
Taylor, James, 37, 59
Taylor, Zachary, 33, 37, 59
Territory of Michigan, xiv, 5n, 22n
Texas, 14, 32, 60n
Thorold, Ont., 64, 71, 75
Timberlake, Margaret O'Neill (or O'Neale), 31
"Torpedo Bureau," 40n
Townsend, Edward D., 35, 51, 52, 84, 101
Towson, Nathaniel, 14, 15n
Tripler, Alice Hunt ("Allie"), 28n, 32, 55
Tripler, Dr. Charles Stuart ("Charlie"), xiv, xvii, xviii, 1, 10, 24, 26–36, 38, 39n, 40–42, 51–56, 58, 60–67, 69–94, 99–101, 103, 106, 109
Tripler, Charles Stuart (b. 1842), 27n, 32

Tripler, Charles Stuart (b. 1846), 54n, 59, 103–108
Tripler, Edgar Maclin, 64n
Tripler, Edward Townsend, 64n, 94
Tripler, Ellen Cass, 39n, 94
Tripler, Ellen Mackintosh, 38n
Tripler, Eunice Montgomery Meigs, 64n, 94
Tripler, Henry Hunt, 76n, 94
Tubman, Harriet, xv
Tyler, John, 27

U

U.S. Army Medical Museum, 82–83
U.S. Capitol, x, 8n, 14, 16, 56, 62, 65, 71
U.S. Sanitary Commission, 69, 70n, 73–74, 80
Utica Female Academy, 23, 24n, 94

V

Vaile, Eugene, 17
Van Buren, Abraham II, 15
Van Buren, John, 11, 15
Van Buren, Martin, 11, 14, 15, 90
Vaughn, Charles Richard, 16
Vesey, Denmark, xv

W

"Walk-in-the-Water," 5
Walker, Mary Edwards, 110, 111
Wallen, Henry D., 42
War Department Building, 9, 65n
War of 1812, x, xv, xvi, 2, 4, 11n, 14, 16n, 24n, 30
Washington, D.C., xiii, xiv, xv, xvii, 5, 6–9, 10n, 12–21, 30, 52, 56, 57–58, 63, 64–65, 66, 68, 70–71, 75, 83, 94, 99, 100, 110, 111
Wayne County Medical Society, 37n
Webster, Daniel, 11
Wellington, Eunice, xv, 6
West Point, 9n, 11n, 30–31, 32n, 34n, 35n, 37n, 38, 39n, 40n, 42n, 51n, 52n, 61, 63, 66n, 67n, 72n, 73n, 82n, 88n, 105n, 108
Wheaton, Walter V., 30
Whistler, Joseph N.G., xv, 88
White House, xiv, 8, 9, 10, 12, 16, 54, 63, 67, 68–69, 71, 87
Williams, Alpheus Starkey, 28n
Wilson, Henry, 65n, 69
Windsor, Ont., 75
Woodbury, Levi, 11, 12
Woodhull, Alfred Alexander, 65, 66
Wool, John E., 15, 16n, 54

Y

Yorktown, Va., 1, 9, 71
Ypsilanti, Mich., 89

Acknowledgments

G rateful appreciation is expressed by the editor to the following, among others: fellow Board members of the Michigan Civil War Association for their dedication to the cause and approval of the publication series; Margaret O'Brien and Matt VanAcker for thematic guidance, research assistance, and manuscript reviews; Dr. Marty Hershock for participation, guidance, and commentary, all volunteered; Brian James Egen for leadership and support to this and future volumes; Jack Lessenberry for supportive input; Dave Dempsey for research and photo support; Lauren Nelson of the Port Huron Museums for assistance on Fort Gratiot and its post hospital; Nadine L. Siak, Public Affairs Specialist, Tripler Army Medical Center, for assistance as to its collections; staff at the Wayne State University Archives at the Reuther Library, at Historic Elmwood Cemetery, and at the Plymouth District Library; and, last in this order but not least, Dr. Charles David Cullen, descendant, for permissions, exchanges, reviews, and much more.

And, of course, borrowing Eunice Hunt Tripler's concluding phrase, for the Good Father I know.